Intermediate Vulkan Programming- Building 3D Graphics

Vulcan Fundamentals, Volume 2

Kameron Hussain and Frahaan Hussain

Published by Sonar Publishing, 2024.

While every precaution has been taken in the preparation of this book, the publisher assumes no responsibility for errors or omissions, or for damages resulting from the use of the information contained herein.

INTERMEDIATE VULKAN PROGRAMMING- BUILDING 3D GRAPHICS

First edition. August 3, 2024.

Copyright © 2024 Kameron Hussain and Frahaan Hussain.

ISBN: 979-8224701971

Written by Kameron Hussain and Frahaan Hussain.

Intermediate Vulkan programming
Building 3D Graphics

SECOND EDITION

Table of Contents

Preface

Welcome to the second edition of our comprehensive guide to Vulkan, the cutting-edge graphics and compute API from the Khronos Group. This book is designed to provide both novice and experienced developers with a deep understanding of Vulkan and its application in real-world scenarios. Each chapter builds on the last, starting from the basics and moving towards advanced topics, ensuring a complete and thorough education in Vulkan's capabilities and usage.

In this edition, we have updated the content to reflect the latest advancements in Vulkan, included new case studies, and expanded the chapters on performance optimization and advanced features. Whether you are interested in game development, scientific visualization, or virtual reality applications, this book offers practical examples and insights to help you harness the power of Vulkan.

We begin with an introduction to the Vulkan API, comparing it with other graphics APIs and guiding you through setting up your development environment. From there, you will dive into the basics of Vulkan, including instance and physical devices, logical devices, and swap chains.

As you progress, you will explore the rendering pipeline, learn how to draw geometry, manage memory, and implement advanced rendering techniques. Chapters on texture mapping, lighting and shading, and performance optimization will help you create visually stunning and efficient applications.

Advanced Vulkan features such as geometry and tessellation shaders, compute shaders, and ray tracing are covered in detail, providing you with the tools to push the boundaries of what is possible with Vulkan.

We also address cross-platform considerations to ensure your applications run smoothly on various platforms.

Finally, we present case studies and real-world applications, showcasing the versatility and power of Vulkan in different domains. By the end of this book, you will have a solid understanding of Vulkan and the confidence to apply it to your own projects.

Thank you for choosing this book as your guide to mastering Vulkan. We hope it inspires you to create amazing applications and pushes the boundaries of your creativity.

Chapter 1: Introduction to Vulkan

Vulkan API Overview

Vulkan is a low-level, cross-platform graphics and compute API developed by the Khronos Group. It is designed to provide high-efficiency, high-performance access to modern GPUs used in a wide variety of devices, from PCs and consoles to mobile phones and embedded platforms.

Unlike its predecessors, Vulkan offers a more explicit control over the GPU, giving developers finer control over resource management, synchronization, and rendering pipelines. This allows for more predictable and optimized performance, particularly in complex and resource-intensive applications.

One of the key features of Vulkan is its ability to handle multiple threads efficiently. Traditional graphics APIs like OpenGL are typically single-threaded, which can become a bottleneck in multi-core systems. Vulkan, however, is designed from the ground up to leverage multi-threading, allowing different parts of the application to execute concurrently and utilize all available CPU cores effectively.

Another significant advantage of Vulkan is its cross-platform nature. Applications developed with Vulkan can run on a wide range of devices and operating systems, including Windows, Linux, macOS, Android, and iOS. This is made possible through the use of platform-specific extensions and the Vulkan loader, which abstracts the platform differences and provides a unified API.

Vulkan also introduces the concept of a command buffer, which allows developers to record a sequence of rendering commands and submit them to the GPU for execution. This is a departure from the immediate mode rendering used in APIs like OpenGL, where commands are executed as they are issued. Command buffers enable more efficient batching of rendering commands, reducing the overhead and improving performance.

To get started with Vulkan, developers need to initialize a Vulkan instance and enumerate the available physical devices. Each physical device represents a GPU, and developers can query the properties and features of each device to select the most suitable one for their application. Once a physical device is selected, a logical device is created, which represents a context for executing commands on the GPU.

Vulkan's memory management model is another area where it differs significantly from other APIs. Developers are responsible for managing memory allocation and deallocation, which provides more control and the potential for optimization. Vulkan also introduces a unified memory model, where the same memory can be used for both CPU and GPU operations, reducing the need for data transfers and improving performance.

One of the challenges of using Vulkan is its verbosity and complexity. The API is designed to be explicit and low-level, which can result in a steep learning curve for developers coming from higher-level APIs. However, this complexity is also what gives Vulkan its power and flexibility, allowing developers to optimize their applications to a degree that is not possible with other APIs.

In conclusion, Vulkan represents a significant step forward in graphics and compute APIs, offering high performance, fine-grained control, and cross-platform capabilities. While it may require more effort to learn and use effectively, the benefits it provides make it a compelling choice for modern graphics and compute applications.

Comparing Vulkan with Other Graphics APIs

When considering graphics APIs, Vulkan stands out due to its low-level nature and explicit control, which contrasts sharply with older, higher-level APIs like OpenGL and Direct3D. Understanding these differences is crucial for developers looking to leverage Vulkan's capabilities to their fullest.

OpenGL vs. Vulkan

OpenGL has been the workhorse of graphics programming for decades, providing a high-level, easy-to-use interface for rendering 2D and 3D graphics. However, its simplicity often comes at the cost of performance and flexibility. OpenGL's immediate mode rendering and state machine architecture can introduce inefficiencies and limit optimization opportunities.

Vulkan, on the other hand, provides a much more explicit control over the GPU. This means that while Vulkan can be more complex and verbose, it offers significant performance benefits, particularly for applications that need to maximize GPU utilization. Vulkan's command buffer system, for instance, allows for efficient batching and parallel execution of rendering commands, which can significantly reduce overhead and improve frame rates.

Direct3D vs. Vulkan

Direct3D, part of Microsoft's DirectX suite, is another widely used graphics API, particularly in the Windows ecosystem. Direct3D has evolved significantly over the years, incorporating many advanced features and optimizations. However, it is platform-specific, primarily targeting Windows and Xbox platforms.

Vulkan's cross-platform capabilities give it a significant advantage in environments where multi-platform support is essential. Vulkan's architecture is designed to be more consistent across different platforms, reducing the need for platform-specific code and allowing developers to maintain a single codebase for multiple targets.

Metal vs. Vulkan

Apple's Metal API shares many similarities with Vulkan, offering low-level access to the GPU and explicit control over rendering and compute operations. However, Metal is exclusive to Apple platforms, limiting its use to macOS, iOS, and tvOS.

Vulkan's broader platform support makes it a more versatile choice for developers targeting multiple operating systems. Additionally, Vulkan's open standard approach, managed by the Khronos Group, ensures a wide range of hardware and software support, further enhancing its appeal for cross-platform development.

High-Level APIs vs. Vulkan

High-level APIs, such as Unity's Scriptable Render Pipeline or Unreal Engine's rendering systems, abstract away much of the complexity involved in graphics programming. These APIs are designed to be user-friendly and accessible, making them ideal for rapid development and prototyping.

While high-level APIs offer ease of use, they often trade off some level of control and optimization potential. Vulkan, with its low-level, explicit control, allows developers to fine-tune every aspect of the rendering pipeline, enabling optimizations that are simply not possible with higher-level abstractions.

Performance Considerations

The primary motivation for using Vulkan over other APIs is performance. Vulkan's design minimizes driver overhead and allows for better multi-threading, which can lead to significant performance improvements in CPU-bound applications. By giving developers direct control over memory management, synchronization, and resource allocation, Vulkan enables a level of optimization that can be crucial for demanding applications such as AAA games, virtual reality, and real-time simulations.

Learning Curve and Development Effort

One of the trade-offs of Vulkan's power and flexibility is its complexity. The API is much more verbose and requires a deeper understanding of the GPU's inner workings compared to higher-level APIs. Developers need to manage many aspects that are handled automatically by other APIs, such as memory allocation, resource synchronization, and error handling.

This steep learning curve can be a barrier to entry, but for developers willing to invest the time and effort, the rewards can be substantial. The explicit control provided by Vulkan allows for more predictable performance and the ability to squeeze every ounce of power from the hardware.

Ecosystem and Tooling

Vulkan's ecosystem has grown significantly since its release, with a wide range of tools, libraries, and frameworks available to support development. Tools like RenderDoc, Vulkan Memory Allocator, and the Vulkan SDK provide invaluable assistance for debugging, profiling, and optimizing Vulkan applications.

Additionally, the community and industry support for Vulkan continues to expand, with contributions from major hardware vendors, game studios, and independent developers. This vibrant ecosystem helps to mitigate some of the challenges associated with Vulkan's complexity, providing resources and support for developers at all levels.

In conclusion, Vulkan offers a unique combination of performance, flexibility, and cross-platform capabilities that set it apart from other graphics APIs. While it may require more effort to master, the potential benefits in terms of performance and control make it an attractive option for developers looking to push the boundaries of what is possible in graphics and compute applications.

Setting Up the Development Environment

Setting up a Vulkan development environment involves several steps, including installing the Vulkan SDK, configuring your build tools, and setting up a project structure. This section will guide you through the process, ensuring you have everything you need to start developing Vulkan applications.

Installing the Vulkan SDK

The first step in setting up your Vulkan development environment is to install the Vulkan SDK. The SDK provides the necessary tools, libraries, and headers to develop Vulkan applications. It includes validation layers, debugging tools, and sample code to help you get started.

1. **Download the SDK**: Visit the LunarG Vulkan SDK website and download the latest version of the SDK for your operating system. The SDK is available for Windows, Linux, and macOS.
2. **Install the SDK**: Follow the installation instructions

provided on the website. The installation process typically involves running an installer or extracting a compressed archive. Make sure to note the installation directory, as you will need to configure your build tools to use the SDK.

Configuring Build Tools

Next, you need to configure your build tools to include the Vulkan SDK headers and link against the Vulkan libraries. This process varies depending on the build system and IDE you are using.

Visual Studio (Windows)

1. **Create a New Project**: Open Visual Studio and create a new C++ project.
2. **Include Vulkan Headers**: In the project properties, add the path to the Vulkan SDK include directory to the "Additional Include Directories" field. This is typically located in the Include subdirectory of the SDK installation directory.
3. **Link Vulkan Libraries**: Add the path to the Vulkan SDK library directory to the "Additional Library Directories" field. Then, add vulkan-1.lib to the "Additional Dependencies" field. This will link your project against the Vulkan runtime library.

CMake (Cross-Platform)

1. **Install CMake**: If you don't already have CMake installed, download and install it from the CMake website.

Create a CMakeLists.txt File: Create a CMakeLists.txt file in your project directory with the following content:

```
cmake_minimum_required(VERSION 3.10)
```

```
project(VulkanApp)

find_package(Vulkan REQUIRED)

add_executable(VulkanApp main.cpp)

target_include_directories(VulkanApp                PRIVATE
${Vulkan_INCLUDE_DIRS})

target_link_libraries(VulkanApp PRIVATE ${Vulkan_LIBRARIES})
```

   1.

```
cmake -S . -B build
```

   1.

```
cmake—build build
```

   1.

Setting Up a Project Structure

A well-organized project structure is essential for managing your Vulkan application's source code, assets, and build configurations. Here is a suggested directory structure for a Vulkan project:

```
VulkanApp/

├── CMakeLists.txt

├── include/

│   └── VulkanApp/

│   └── VulkanApp.h

├── src/

│   └── VulkanApp/
```

```
|    └──── main.cpp
├──── shaders/
|    └──── shader.vert
|    └──── shader.frag
└──── assets/
└──── textures/
└──── models/
```

- include/: Contains header files.

- src/: Contains source files.

- shaders/: Contains shader source files.

- assets/: Contains assets such as textures and models.

Writing Your First Vulkan Program

With your development environment set up, you can now write your first Vulkan program. Start by including the Vulkan headers and initializing a Vulkan instance. Here is a simple example to get you started:

```cpp
#include <vulkan/vulkan.h>

#include <iostream>

int main() {

VkInstance instance;

VkApplicationInfo appInfo{};
```

```cpp
appInfo.sType = VK_STRUCTURE_TYPE_APPLICATION_INFO;

appInfo.pApplicationName = "Hello Vulkan";

appInfo.applicationVersion = VK_MAKE_VERSION(1, 0, 0);

appInfo.pEngineName = "No Engine";

appInfo.engineVersion = VK_MAKE_VERSION(1, 0, 0);

appInfo.apiVersion = VK_API_VERSION_1_0;

VkInstanceCreateInfo createInfo{};

createInfo.sType = VK_STRUCTURE_TYPE_INSTANCE_CREATE_INFO;

createInfo.pApplicationInfo = &appInfo;

if (vkCreateInstance(&createInfo, nullptr, &instance) != VK_SUCCESS) {

std::cerr << "Failed to create Vulkan instance!" << std::endl;

return -1;

}

std::cout << "Vulkan instance created successfully!" << std::endl;

vkDestroyInstance(instance, nullptr);

return 0;

}
```

This code initializes a Vulkan instance and then immediately destroys it. It's a minimal example, but it demonstrates the basic setup required to start using Vulkan.

Validation Layers and Debugging

To ensure your Vulkan application runs correctly and efficiently, it's important to use validation layers and debugging tools. Validation layers check your code for errors and provide detailed diagnostic information.

```cpp
const std::vector<const char*> validationLayers = {

"VK_LAYER_KHRONOS_validation"

};

VkInstanceCreateInfo createInfo{};

createInfo.sType                                    = VK_STRUCTURE_TYPE_INSTANCE_CREATE_INFO;

createInfo.pApplicationInfo = &appInfo;

if (!validationLayers.empty()) {

createInfo.enabledLayerCount                         = static_cast<uint32_t>(validationLayers.size());

createInfo.ppEnabledLayerNames = validationLayers.data();

} else {

createInfo.enabledLayerCount = 0;

}
```

1.

2. **Use Debugging Tools**: Tools like RenderDoc and the Vulkan Validation Layer can help you diagnose and fix issues in your Vulkan code. These tools provide insights into the rendering process and highlight potential problems.

By following these steps, you'll have a solid foundation for developing Vulkan applications. With the Vulkan SDK installed, your build tools configured, and a well-organized project structure, you're ready to dive deeper into Vulkan and explore its powerful features.

Chapter 2: Vulkan Basics

Instance and Physical Devices

In Vulkan, the instance is the foundation of your application. It represents the connection between your application and the Vulkan library. The instance is responsible for querying and selecting physical devices, which are the actual hardware components that will execute your rendering commands.

Creating an instance involves specifying application information and desired extensions. The application information is not mandatory, but it can help with debugging and profiling. Extensions are optional features that can enhance the functionality of Vulkan.

```
VkApplicationInfo appInfo = {};

appInfo.sType                                        =
VK_STRUCTURE_TYPE_APPLICATION_INFO;

appInfo.pApplicationName = "VulkanApp";

appInfo.applicationVersion = VK_MAKE_VERSION(1, 0, 0);

appInfo.pEngineName = "No Engine";

appInfo.engineVersion = VK_MAKE_VERSION(1, 0, 0);

appInfo.apiVersion = VK_API_VERSION_1_0;

VkInstanceCreateInfo createInfo = {};

createInfo.sType                                     =
VK_STRUCTURE_TYPE_INSTANCE_CREATE_INFO;

createInfo.pApplicationInfo = &appInfo;
```

```cpp
if (vkCreateInstance(&createInfo, nullptr, &instance) != VK_SUCCESS) {

throw std::runtime_error("failed to create instance!");

}
```

Once the instance is created, you can enumerate physical devices. Each physical device represents a GPU in the system. Vulkan provides a function to get a list of all available physical devices.

```cpp
uint32_t deviceCount = 0;

vkEnumeratePhysicalDevices(instance, &deviceCount, nullptr);

if (deviceCount == 0) {

throw std::runtime_error("failed to find GPUs with Vulkan support!");

}

std::vector<VkPhysicalDevice> devices(deviceCount);

vkEnumeratePhysicalDevices(instance, &deviceCount, devices.data());
```

After enumerating the physical devices, you can select one based on your criteria. Common criteria include checking for support of necessary features, extension availability, and performance characteristics.

```cpp
VkPhysicalDevice physicalDevice = VK_NULL_HANDLE;

for (const auto& device : devices) {

if (isDeviceSuitable(device)) {
```

```cpp
physicalDevice = device;

break;

}

}

if (physicalDevice == VK_NULL_HANDLE) {

throw std::runtime_error("failed to find a suitable GPU!");

}
```

The function isDeviceSuitable should evaluate the physical device based on your application's needs. This function typically checks for queue family support, required extensions, and specific features.

```cpp
bool isDeviceSuitable(VkPhysicalDevice device) {

VkPhysicalDeviceProperties deviceProperties;

VkPhysicalDeviceFeatures deviceFeatures;

vkGetPhysicalDeviceProperties(device, &deviceProperties);

vkGetPhysicalDeviceFeatures(device, &deviceFeatures);

bool extensionsSupported = checkDeviceExtensionSupport(device);

return                    deviceProperties.deviceType                    ==
VK_PHYSICAL_DEVICE_TYPE_DISCRETE_GPU &&

deviceFeatures.geometryShader && extensionsSupported;

}
```

In isDeviceSuitable, checkDeviceExtensionSupport should verify that the physical device supports all necessary Vulkan extensions.

```cpp
bool checkDeviceExtensionSupport(VkPhysicalDevice device) {

uint32_t extensionCount;

vkEnumerateDeviceExtensionProperties(device,           nullptr,
&extensionCount, nullptr);

std::vector<VkExtensionProperties>
availableExtensions(extensionCount);

vkEnumerateDeviceExtensionProperties(device,           nullptr,
&extensionCount, availableExtensions.data());

std::set<std::string>    requiredExtensions(deviceExtensions.begin(),
deviceExtensions.end());

for (const auto& extension : availableExtensions) {

requiredExtensions.erase(extension.extensionName);

}

return requiredExtensions.empty();

}
```

This setup ensures that you select a physical device that meets your application's requirements. Once you have a suitable physical device, you can proceed to create logical devices and queues to manage your rendering operations.

Understanding the instance and physical devices in Vulkan is crucial as it sets the stage for subsequent steps, such as creating logical devices and setting up the rendering pipeline.

Logical Devices and Queues

Once a suitable physical device is selected, the next step is to create a logical device. A logical device serves as an interface to interact with the physical device and provides access to various queues that handle different types of operations.

To create a logical device, you need to specify the queue families and their respective priorities. Queue families represent different types of operations, such as graphics, compute, and transfer. Each queue family can have multiple queues, which are used to submit commands for execution.

```cpp
QueueFamilyIndices indices = findQueueFamilies(physicalDevice);

float queuePriority = 1.0f;

VkDeviceQueueCreateInfo queueCreateInfo = {};

queueCreateInfo.sType                                         =
VK_STRUCTURE_TYPE_DEVICE_QUEUE_CREATE_INFO;

queueCreateInfo.queueFamilyIndex = indices.graphicsFamily.value();

queueCreateInfo.queueCount = 1;

queueCreateInfo.pQueuePriorities = &queuePriority;

VkPhysicalDeviceFeatures deviceFeatures = {};

VkDeviceCreateInfo createInfo = {};

createInfo.sType                                             =
VK_STRUCTURE_TYPE_DEVICE_CREATE_INFO;

createInfo.pQueueCreateInfos = &queueCreateInfo;

createInfo.queueCreateInfoCount = 1;
```

```cpp
createInfo.pEnabledFeatures = &deviceFeatures;

if (vkCreateDevice(physicalDevice, &createInfo, nullptr, &device) !=
VK_SUCCESS) {

throw std::runtime_error("failed to create logical device!");

}
```

The findQueueFamilies function identifies the indices of the queue families that support the required operations. For example, a graphics queue family is necessary for rendering tasks.

```cpp
struct QueueFamilyIndices {

std::optional<uint32_t> graphicsFamily;

std::optional<uint32_t> presentFamily;

bool isComplete() {

return graphicsFamily.has_value() && presentFamily.has_value();

}

};

QueueFamilyIndices findQueueFamilies(VkPhysicalDevice device) {

QueueFamilyIndices indices;

uint32_t queueFamilyCount = 0;

vkGetPhysicalDeviceQueueFamilyProperties(device,
&queueFamilyCount, nullptr);

std::vector<VkQueueFamilyProperties>
queueFamilies(queueFamilyCount);
```

```cpp
vkGetPhysicalDeviceQueueFamilyProperties(device,
&queueFamilyCount, queueFamilies.data());

int i = 0;

for (const auto& queueFamily : queueFamilies) {

if (queueFamily.queueFlags & VK_QUEUE_GRAPHICS_BIT) {

indices.graphicsFamily = i;

}

VkBool32 presentSupport = false;

vkGetPhysicalDeviceSurfaceSupportKHR(device,        i,        surface,
&presentSupport);

if (presentSupport) {

indices.presentFamily = i;

}

if (indices.isComplete()) {

break;

}

i++;

}

return indices;

}
```

After creating the logical device, you can retrieve the queue handles. These handles are used to submit command buffers for execution on the GPU.

VkQueue graphicsQueue;

vkGetDeviceQueue(device, indices.graphicsFamily.value(), 0, &graphicsQueue);

VkQueue presentQueue;

vkGetDeviceQueue(device, indices.presentFamily.value(), 0, &presentQueue);

Having the logical device and queues set up is crucial as it allows your application to interact with the GPU and perform rendering tasks. Logical devices provide a layer of abstraction over the physical hardware, making it easier to manage and optimize rendering operations.

Logical devices and queues form the backbone of Vulkan's execution model. They facilitate the submission of commands to the GPU and enable efficient management of rendering tasks. Understanding their creation and usage is essential for leveraging Vulkan's capabilities effectively.

Swap Chains and Presentation

Swap chains are a critical component in Vulkan for rendering images to the screen. They manage the sequence of images that are presented to the display and handle synchronization between the GPU and the display hardware. Setting up a swap chain involves several steps, including querying support details, choosing surface formats, and creating the swap chain itself.

First, you need to query the swap chain support details for the physical device. This includes checking the capabilities, supported surface formats, and available presentation modes.

```
SwapChainSupportDetails
querySwapChainSupport(VkPhysicalDevice device) {

SwapChainSupportDetails details;

vkGetPhysicalDeviceSurfaceCapabilitiesKHR(device,        surface,
&details.capabilities);

uint32_t formatCount;

vkGetPhysicalDeviceSurfaceFormatsKHR(device,        surface,
&formatCount, nullptr);

if (formatCount != 0) {

details.formats.resize(formatCount);

vkGetPhysicalDeviceSurfaceFormatsKHR(device,        surface,
&formatCount, details.formats.data());

}

uint32_t presentModeCount;

vkGetPhysicalDeviceSurfacePresentModesKHR(device,        surface,
&presentModeCount, nullptr);

if (presentModeCount != 0) {

details.presentModes.resize(presentModeCount);

vkGetPhysicalDeviceSurfacePresentModesKHR(device,        surface,
&presentModeCount, details.presentModes.data());
```

```cpp
}

return details;

}
```

With the swap chain support details in hand, you can choose the best surface format, presentation mode, and swap extent for your application.

```cpp
VkSurfaceFormatKHR chooseSwapSurfaceFormat(const std::vector<VkSurfaceFormatKHR>& availableFormats) {

for (const auto& availableFormat : availableFormats) {

if (availableFormat.format == VK_FORMAT_B8G8R8A8_SRGB && availableFormat.colorSpace == VK_COLOR_SPACE_SRGB_NONLINEAR_KHR) {

return availableFormat;

}

}

return availableFormats[0];

}

VkPresentModeKHR chooseSwapPresentMode(const std::vector<VkPresentModeKHR>& availablePresentModes) {

for (const auto& availablePresentMode : availablePresentModes) {

if (availablePresentMode == VK_PRESENT_MODE_MAILBOX_KHR) {

return availablePresentMode;
```

```cpp
}

}

return VK_PRESENT_MODE_FIFO_KHR;

}

VkExtent2D chooseSwapExtent(const VkSurfaceCapabilitiesKHR&
capabilities) {

if (capabilities.currentExtent.width != UINT32_MAX) {

return capabilities.currentExtent;

} else {

VkExtent2D actualExtent = { WIDTH, HEIGHT };

actualExtent.width = std::max(capabilities.minImageExtent.width,
std::min(capabilities.maxImageExtent.width, actualExtent.width));

actualExtent.height = std::max(capabilities.minImageExtent.height,
std::min(capabilities.maxImageExtent.height, actualExtent.height));

return actualExtent;

}

}
```

Once you have chosen the format, mode, and extent, you can create the swap chain. This involves specifying the number of images, their usage, and the sharing mode.

```cpp
VkSwapchainCreateInfoKHR createInfo = {};
```

```cpp
createInfo.sType = VK_STRUCTURE_TYPE_SWAPCHAIN_CREATE_INFO_KHR;

createInfo.surface = surface;

VkSurfaceFormatKHR surfaceFormat = chooseSwapSurfaceFormat(swapChainSupport.formats);

VkPresentModeKHR presentMode = chooseSwapPresentMode(swapChainSupport.presentModes);

VkExtent2D extent = chooseSwapExtent(swapChainSupport.capabilities);

createInfo.minImageCount = swapChainSupport.capabilities.minImageCount + 1;

if (swapChainSupport.capabilities.maxImageCount > 0 && createInfo.minImageCount > swapChainSupport.capabilities.maxImageCount) {

createInfo.minImageCount = swapChainSupport.capabilities.maxImageCount;

}

createInfo.imageFormat = surfaceFormat.format;

createInfo.imageColorSpace = surfaceFormat.colorSpace;

createInfo.imageExtent = extent;

createInfo.imageArrayLayers = 1;

createInfo.imageUsage = VK_IMAGE_USAGE_COLOR_ATTACHMENT_BIT;

QueueFamilyIndices indices = findQueueFamilies(physicalDevice);
```

```cpp
uint32_t queueFamilyIndices[] = { indices.graphicsFamily.value(),
indices.presentFamily.value() };

if (indices.graphicsFamily != indices.presentFamily) {

createInfo.imageSharingMode                                    =
VK_SHARING_MODE_CONCURRENT;

createInfo.queueFamilyIndexCount = 2;

createInfo.pQueueFamilyIndices = queueFamilyIndices;

} else {

createInfo.imageSharingMode                                    =
VK_SHARING_MODE_EXCLUSIVE;

createInfo.queueFamilyIndexCount = 0; // Optional

createInfo.pQueueFamilyIndices = nullptr; // Optional

}

createInfo.preTransform                                        =
swapChainSupport.capabilities.currentTransform;

createInfo.compositeAlpha                                      =
VK_COMPOSITE_ALPHA_OPAQUE_BIT_KHR;

createInfo.presentMode = presentMode;

createInfo.clipped = VK_TRUE;

createInfo.oldSwapchain = VK_NULL_HANDLE;

if    (vkCreateSwapchainKHR(device,       &createInfo,    nullptr,
&swapChain) != VK_SUCCESS) {
```

```
throw std::runtime_error("failed to create swap chain!");
```

```
}
```

After creating the swap chain, you need to retrieve the swap chain images and create image views for each image. Image views provide a way to access the images and are used in the rendering pipeline.

```
vkGetSwapchainImagesKHR(device, swapChain, &imageCount, nullptr);
```

```
swapChainImages.resize(imageCount);
```

```
vkGetSwapchainImagesKHR(device, swapChain, &imageCount, swapChainImages.data());
```

```
swapChainImageFormat = surfaceFormat.format;
```

```
swapChainExtent = extent;
```

```
swapChainImageViews.resize(swapChainImages.size());
```

```
for (size_t i = 0; i < swapChainImages.size(); i++) {
```

```
VkImageViewCreateInfo createInfo = {};
```

```
createInfo.sType = VK_STRUCTURE_TYPE_IMAGE_VIEW_CREATE_INFO;
```

```
createInfo.image = swapChainImages[i];
```

```
createInfo.viewType = VK_IMAGE_VIEW_TYPE_2D;
```

```
createInfo.format = swapChainImageFormat;
```

```
createInfo.components.r = VK_COMPONENT_SWIZZLE_IDENTITY;
```

```
createInfo.components.g                                          =
VK_COMPONENT_SWIZZLE_IDENTITY;

createInfo.components.b                                          =
VK_COMPONENT_SWIZZLE_IDENTITY;

createInfo.components.a                                          =
VK_COMPONENT_SWIZZLE_IDENTITY;

createInfo.subresourceRange.aspectMask                           =
VK_IMAGE_ASPECT_COLOR_BIT;

createInfo.subresourceRange.baseMipLevel = 0;

createInfo.subresourceRange.levelCount = 1;

createInfo.subresourceRange.baseArrayLayer = 0;

createInfo.subresourceRange.layerCount = 1;

if      (vkCreateImageView(device,        &createInfo,        nullptr,
&swapChainImageViews[i]) != VK_SUCCESS) {

throw std::runtime_error("failed to create image views!");

}

}
```

Setting up the swap chain is essential for presenting rendered images to the screen. It handles the complexity of managing multiple images, synchronization, and interaction with the display hardware, ensuring smooth and efficient rendering.

Understanding the creation and configuration of swap chains is fundamental to developing Vulkan applications that can render and display graphics effectively.

Chapter 3: Rendering Pipeline

Vulkan Pipeline Architecture

The Vulkan pipeline architecture is a comprehensive and modular system that controls how data flows from the application to the GPU and eventually to the screen. It is designed to provide developers with fine-grained control over the rendering process, offering flexibility and efficiency. Unlike fixed-function pipelines of older graphics APIs, Vulkan's pipeline is highly configurable and consists of multiple stages, each with specific responsibilities.

At a high level, the Vulkan pipeline is divided into several stages: input assembly, vertex shading, tessellation (optional), geometry shading (optional), rasterization, fragment shading, and output merging. Each stage has a well-defined role, allowing developers to insert custom shaders and configurations at various points to achieve the desired rendering effects.

Input Assembly

The input assembly stage is responsible for gathering vertex data from buffers and assembling it into geometric primitives like points, lines, and triangles. This stage is highly configurable, allowing developers to specify the format and layout of vertex data.

Vertex Shading

In the vertex shading stage, each vertex is processed individually by a vertex shader. The vertex shader is a programmable unit that can perform various transformations and calculations on vertex attributes, such as position, color, and texture coordinates. This stage is crucial for operations like model transformations and lighting calculations.

Tessellation

Tessellation is an optional stage that subdivides geometric primitives into finer pieces, allowing for detailed and smooth surfaces. It consists of two programmable stages: the tessellation control shader and the tessellation evaluation shader. These shaders control the level of tessellation and the shape of the tessellated geometry.

Geometry Shading

The geometry shading stage, also optional, processes entire primitives (such as triangles) and can generate new geometry or modify existing geometry. The geometry shader operates after the vertex and tessellation stages and before rasterization. It is useful for tasks like dynamic mesh generation and culling.

Rasterization

The rasterization stage converts geometric primitives into fragments, which correspond to pixels on the screen. This stage performs tasks like clipping, perspective division, and viewport transformation. Rasterization is a fixed-function stage, meaning it does not involve custom shaders but can be configured with various parameters.

Fragment Shading

In the fragment shading stage, each fragment generated by rasterization is processed by a fragment shader. The fragment shader determines the color, depth, and other attributes of each fragment. This stage is essential for implementing per-pixel effects like texturing, lighting, and shadowing.

Output Merging

The final stage of the pipeline is output merging, where fragments are combined to produce the final image. This stage includes operations like depth testing, blending, and writing to the framebuffer. The output merging stage ensures that the fragments are correctly combined based on their depth and other attributes.

Pipeline Configuration

Creating a Vulkan pipeline involves defining the configuration for each stage and linking them together. This process is done through pipeline state objects (PSOs), which encapsulate the configuration and state of the entire pipeline. PSOs are immutable once created, which means changes require creating new PSOs. This immutability ensures consistency and performance.

Code Example: Creating a Basic Pipeline

```cpp
VkPipelineShaderStageCreateInfo shaderStages[] = {vertexShaderStageInfo, fragmentShaderStageInfo};

VkPipelineVertexInputStateCreateInfo vertexInputInfo = {};

vertexInputInfo.sType = VK_STRUCTURE_TYPE_PIPELINE_VERTEX_INPUT_STATE_C

vertexInputInfo.vertexBindingDescriptionCount = 1;

vertexInputInfo.pVertexBindingDescriptions = &bindingDescription;

vertexInputInfo.vertexAttributeDescriptionCount = static_cast<uint32_t>(attributeDescriptions.size());

vertexInputInfo.pVertexAttributeDescriptions = attributeDescriptions.data();
```

```cpp
VkPipelineInputAssemblyStateCreateInfo inputAssembly = {};

inputAssembly.sType                                    =
VK_STRUCTURE_TYPE_PIPELINE_INPUT_ASSEMBLY_STATE_CF

inputAssembly.topology                                 =
VK_PRIMITIVE_TOPOLOGY_TRIANGLE_LIST;

inputAssembly.primitiveRestartEnable = VK_FALSE;

VkPipelineRasterizationStateCreateInfo rasterizer = {};

rasterizer.sType                                       =
VK_STRUCTURE_TYPE_PIPELINE_RASTERIZATION_STATE_CRE

rasterizer.depthClampEnable = VK_FALSE;

rasterizer.rasterizerDiscardEnable = VK_FALSE;

rasterizer.polygonMode = VK_POLYGON_MODE_FILL;

rasterizer.lineWidth = 1.0f;

rasterizer.cullMode = VK_CULL_MODE_BACK_BIT;

rasterizer.frontFace = VK_FRONT_FACE_CLOCKWISE;

rasterizer.depthBiasEnable = VK_FALSE;

VkPipelineMultisampleStateCreateInfo multisampling = {};

multisampling.sType                                    =
VK_STRUCTURE_TYPE_PIPELINE_MULTISAMPLE_STATE_CREA

multisampling.sampleShadingEnable = VK_FALSE;

multisampling.rasterizationSamples                     =
VK_SAMPLE_COUNT_1_BIT;
```

```cpp
VkPipelineColorBlendAttachmentState colorBlendAttachment = {};

colorBlendAttachment.colorWriteMask               =
VK_COLOR_COMPONENT_R_BIT                           |
VK_COLOR_COMPONENT_G_BIT                           |
VK_COLOR_COMPONENT_B_BIT                           |
VK_COLOR_COMPONENT_A_BIT;

colorBlendAttachment.blendEnable = VK_FALSE;

VkPipelineColorBlendStateCreateInfo colorBlending = {};

colorBlending.sType                               =
VK_STRUCTURE_TYPE_PIPELINE_COLOR_BLEND_STATE_CF

colorBlending.logicOpEnable = VK_FALSE;

colorBlending.logicOp = VK_LOGIC_OP_COPY;

colorBlending.attachmentCount = 1;

colorBlending.pAttachments = &colorBlendAttachment;

colorBlending.blendConstants[0] = 0.0f;

colorBlending.blendConstants[1] = 0.0f;

colorBlending.blendConstants[2] = 0.0f;

colorBlending.blendConstants[3] = 0.0f;

VkPipelineLayoutCreateInfo pipelineLayoutInfo = {};

pipelineLayoutInfo.sType                          =
VK_STRUCTURE_TYPE_PIPELINE_LAYOUT_CREATE_INFO;

if (vkCreatePipelineLayout(device, &pipelineLayoutInfo, nullptr,
&pipelineLayout) != VK_SUCCESS) {
```

```cpp
throw std::runtime_error("failed to create pipeline layout!");
}

VkGraphicsPipelineCreateInfo pipelineInfo = {};

pipelineInfo.sType = VK_STRUCTURE_TYPE_GRAPHICS_PIPELINE_CREATE_INFO;

pipelineInfo.stageCount = 2;

pipelineInfo.pStages = shaderStages;

pipelineInfo.pVertexInputState = &vertexInputInfo;

pipelineInfo.pInputAssemblyState = &inputAssembly;

pipelineInfo.pViewportState = &viewportState;

pipelineInfo.pRasterizationState = &rasterizer;

pipelineInfo.pMultisampleState = &multisampling;

pipelineInfo.pDepthStencilState = nullptr;

pipelineInfo.pColorBlendState = &colorBlending;

pipelineInfo.pDynamicState = nullptr;

pipelineInfo.layout = pipelineLayout;

pipelineInfo.renderPass = renderPass;

pipelineInfo.subpass = 0;

if (vkCreateGraphicsPipelines(device, VK_NULL_HANDLE, 1, &pipelineInfo, nullptr, &graphicsPipeline) != VK_SUCCESS) {

throw std::runtime_error("failed to create graphics pipeline!");
```

```
}
```

This code snippet demonstrates the creation of a basic Vulkan graphics pipeline. It sets up the necessary structures and configurations for each pipeline stage, including shader stages, vertex input, input assembly, rasterization, multisampling, and color blending. Finally, it creates the graphics pipeline using vkCreateGraphicsPipelines.

Understanding the Vulkan pipeline architecture and how to configure it is fundamental to harnessing the power and flexibility of Vulkan. By defining custom shaders and configurations at each stage, developers can create sophisticated rendering effects and optimize performance for their applications.

Configuring the Pipeline

Configuring the Vulkan pipeline involves setting up various pipeline stages and their respective state objects. Each stage requires specific configurations to ensure the pipeline operates correctly and efficiently. The process includes defining shader stages, vertex input state, input assembly state, viewport and scissor state, rasterization state, multisample state, depth and stencil state, and color blend state.

Shader Stages

Shader stages are critical components of the Vulkan pipeline. They are responsible for executing custom code to process vertex and fragment data. Each shader stage requires a corresponding shader module and stage-specific information.

```
VkPipelineShaderStageCreateInfo shaderStages[2] = {};

shaderStages[0].sType                                    =
VK_STRUCTURE_TYPE_PIPELINE_SHADER_STAGE_CREATE_
```

```cpp
shaderStages[0].stage = VK_SHADER_STAGE_VERTEX_BIT;

shaderStages[0].module = vertexShaderModule;

shaderStages[0].pName = "main";

shaderStages[1].sType                                        =
VK_STRUCTURE_TYPE_PIPELINE_SHADER_STAGE_CREATE_IN

shaderStages[1].stage                                        =
VK_SHADER_STAGE_FRAGMENT_BIT;

shaderStages[1].module = fragmentShaderModule;

shaderStages[1].pName = "main";
```

Vertex Input State

The vertex input state describes the format of the vertex data passed to the vertex shader. This includes binding descriptions and attribute descriptions.

```cpp
VkPipelineVertexInputStateCreateInfo vertexInputInfo = {};

vertexInputInfo.sType                                        =
VK_STRUCTURE_TYPE_PIPELINE_VERTEX_INPUT_STATE_CRE

vertexInputInfo.vertexBindingDescriptionCount = 1;

vertexInputInfo.pVertexBindingDescriptions = &bindingDescription;

vertexInputInfo.vertexAttributeDescriptionCount              =
static_cast<uint32_t>(attributeDescriptions.size());

vertexInputInfo.pVertexAttributeDescriptions                 =
attributeDescriptions.data();
```

Input Assembly State

The input assembly state specifies the type of geometric primitives to assemble from the vertex data. It also controls whether primitive restart is enabled.

```
VkPipelineInputAssemblyStateCreateInfo inputAssembly = {};

inputAssembly.sType                                    =
VK_STRUCTURE_TYPE_PIPELINE_INPUT_ASSEMBLY_STATE_

inputAssembly.topology                                 =
VK_PRIMITIVE_TOPOLOGY_TRIANGLE_LIST;

inputAssembly.primitiveRestartEnable = VK_FALSE;
```

Viewport and Scissor State

The viewport and scissor state define the viewport transformations and scissor rectangles used during rasterization.

```
VkPipelineViewportStateCreateInfo viewportState = {};

viewportState.sType                                    =
VK_STRUCTURE_TYPE_PIPELINE_VIEWPORT_STATE_CREAT

viewportState.viewportCount = 1;

viewportState.pViewports = &viewport;

viewportState.scissorCount = 1;

viewportState.pScissors = &scissor;
```

Rasterization State

The rasterization state configures how polygons are rasterized. This includes settings for polygon mode, culling, front face, depth bias, and line width.

```cpp
VkPipelineRasterizationStateCreateInfo rasterizer = {};

rasterizer.sType =
VK_STRUCTURE_TYPE_PIPELINE_RASTERIZATION_STATE_CRE

rasterizer.depthClampEnable = VK_FALSE;

rasterizer.rasterizerDiscardEnable = VK_FALSE;

rasterizer.polygonMode = VK_POLYGON_MODE_FILL;

rasterizer.lineWidth = 1.0f;

rasterizer.cullMode = VK_CULL_MODE_BACK_BIT;

rasterizer.frontFace = VK_FRONT_FACE_CLOCKWISE;

rasterizer.depthBiasEnable = VK_FALSE;
```

Multisample State

The multisample state configures multisampling, which is used for anti-aliasing. This includes settings for sample count and sample shading.

```cpp
VkPipelineMultisampleStateCreateInfo multisampling = {};

multisampling.sType =
VK_STRUCTURE_TYPE_PIPELINE_MULTISAMPLE_STATE_CREA

multisampling.sampleShadingEnable = VK_FALSE;
```

```
multisampling.rasterizationSamples                              =
VK_SAMPLE_COUNT_1_BIT;
```

Depth and Stencil State

The depth and stencil state configures depth testing and stencil testing. This stage is crucial for implementing depth-based rendering techniques.

```
VkPipelineDepthStencilStateCreateInfo depthStencil = {};

depthStencil.sType                                             =
VK_STRUCTURE_TYPE_PIPELINE_DEPTH_STENCIL_STATE_C

depthStencil.depthTestEnable = VK_TRUE;

depthStencil.depthWriteEnable = VK_TRUE;

depthStencil.depthCompareOp = VK_COMPARE_OP_LESS;

depthStencil.depthBoundsTestEnable = VK_FALSE;

depthStencil.stencilTestEnable = VK_FALSE;
```

Color Blend State

The color blend state configures blending operations, which determine how fragment colors are combined with existing colors in the framebuffer.

```
VkPipelineColorBlendAttachmentState colorBlendAttachment = {};

colorBlendAttachment.colorWriteMask                           =
VK_COLOR_COMPONENT_R_BIT                                        |
VK_COLOR_COMPONENT_G_BIT                                        |
VK_COLOR_COMPONENT_B_BIT                                        |
VK_COLOR_COMPONENT_A_BIT;
```

```
colorBlendAttachment.blendEnable = VK_FALSE;

VkPipelineColorBlendStateCreateInfo colorBlending = {};

colorBlending.sType = VK_STRUCTURE_TYPE_PIPELINE_COLOR_BLEND_STATE_CREA

colorBlending.logicOpEnable = VK_FALSE;

colorBlending.logicOp = VK_LOGIC_OP_COPY;

colorBlending.attachmentCount = 1;

colorBlending.pAttachments = &colorBlendAttachment;

colorBlending.blendConstants[0] = 0.0f;

colorBlending.blendConstants[1] = 0.0f;

colorBlending.blendConstants[2] = 0.0f;

colorBlending.blendConstants[3] = 0.0f;
```

Pipeline Layout

The pipeline layout defines the interface between the pipeline and the shader stages. This includes descriptor set layouts and push constants.

```
VkPipelineLayoutCreateInfo pipelineLayoutInfo = {};

pipelineLayoutInfo.sType = VK_STRUCTURE_TYPE_PIPELINE_LAYOUT_CREATE_INFO;

pipelineLayoutInfo.setLayoutCount = 1;

pipelineLayoutInfo.pSetLayouts = &descriptorSetLayout;

pipelineLayoutInfo.pushConstantRangeCount = 0;
```

```cpp
if (vkCreatePipelineLayout(device, &pipelineLayoutInfo, nullptr,
&pipelineLayout) != VK_SUCCESS) {

throw std::runtime_error("failed to create pipeline layout!");

}
```

Creating the Graphics Pipeline

After defining the configurations for each stage, the graphics pipeline can be created. The vkCreateGraphicsPipelines function takes a VkGraphicsPipelineCreateInfo structure that encapsulates all the stage configurations.

```cpp
VkGraphicsPipelineCreateInfo pipelineInfo = {};

pipelineInfo.sType = VK_STRUCTURE_TYPE_GRAPHICS_PIPELINE_CREATE_INFO

pipelineInfo.stageCount = 2;

pipelineInfo.pStages = shaderStages;

pipelineInfo.pVertexInputState = &vertexInputInfo;

pipelineInfo.pInputAssemblyState = &inputAssembly;

pipelineInfo.pViewportState = &viewportState;

pipelineInfo.pRasterizationState = &rasterizer;

pipelineInfo.pMultisampleState = &multisampling;

pipelineInfo.pDepthStencilState = &depthStencil;

pipelineInfo.pColorBlendState = &colorBlending;

pipelineInfo.layout = pipelineLayout;
```

```
pipelineInfo.renderPass = renderPass;

pipelineInfo.subpass = 0;

if  (vkCreateGraphicsPipelines(device,  VK_NULL_HANDLE,  1,
&pipelineInfo, nullptr, &graphicsPipeline) != VK_SUCCESS) {

throw std::runtime_error("failed to create graphics pipeline!");

}
```

By configuring the pipeline correctly, developers can ensure efficient and effective rendering of graphics using Vulkan. The flexibility of the pipeline architecture allows for a wide range of rendering techniques and optimizations.

Shaders and Shader Modules

Shaders are small programs that run on the GPU and are responsible for various stages of the graphics pipeline. In Vulkan, shaders are written in GLSL (OpenGL Shading Language) or HLSL (High-Level Shading Language) and then compiled into SPIR-V (Standard Portable Intermediate Representation) bytecode. The SPIR-V format is used by Vulkan for its cross-platform compatibility and performance benefits.

Shader Types

Vulkan supports several types of shaders, each corresponding to a stage in the graphics pipeline:

- **Vertex Shader**: Processes each vertex and is responsible for transforming vertex positions, calculating per-vertex lighting, and passing data to the next stage.

- **Fragment Shader**: Processes each fragment (potential pixel) and determines its color and other attributes. This stage is essential for texturing, shading, and other per-pixel effects.

- **Tessellation Control and Evaluation Shaders**: Used for tessellation, which subdivides geometric primitives into finer pieces.

- **Geometry Shader**: Processes entire primitives (such as triangles) and can generate or modify geometry.

- **Compute Shader**: A general-purpose shader that performs computations not necessarily related to graphics.

Creating Shader Modules

To use shaders in a Vulkan application, they must first be compiled into SPIR-V and then loaded into Vulkan as shader modules. The following example demonstrates how to create a shader module:

```cpp
VkShaderModule createShaderModule(const std::vector<char>& code) {

VkShaderModuleCreateInfo createInfo = {};

createInfo.sType = VK_STRUCTURE_TYPE_SHADER_MODULE_CREATE_INFO;

createInfo.codeSize = code.size();

createInfo.pCode = reinterpret_cast<const uint32_t*>(code.data());

VkShaderModule shaderModule;
```

```cpp
if        (vkCreateShaderModule(device,        &createInfo,        nullptr,
&shaderModule) != VK_SUCCESS) {

throw std::runtime_error("failed to create shader module!");

}

return shaderModule;

}
```

Loading and Using Shaders

After creating shader modules, they need to be associated with the appropriate stages in the pipeline. This is done using VkPipelineShaderStageCreateInfo structures.

```cpp
VkPipelineShaderStageCreateInfo vertShaderStageInfo = {};

vertShaderStageInfo.sType                                              =
VK_STRUCTURE_TYPE_PIPELINE_SHADER_STAGE_CREATE_IN

vertShaderStageInfo.stage                                             =
VK_SHADER_STAGE_VERTEX_BIT;

vertShaderStageInfo.module = vertShaderModule;

vertShaderStageInfo.pName = "main";

VkPipelineShaderStageCreateInfo fragShaderStageInfo = {};

fragShaderStageInfo.sType                                             =
VK_STRUCTURE_TYPE_PIPELINE_SHADER_STAGE_CREATE_IN

fragShaderStageInfo.stage                                            =
VK_SHADER_STAGE_FRAGMENT_BIT;

fragShaderStageInfo.module = fragShaderModule;
```

```
fragShaderStageInfo.pName = "main";
```

Shader Code Example

Here is an example of a simple vertex shader written in GLSL:

```glsl
#version 450

layout(location = 0) in vec2 inPosition;

layout(location = 1) in vec3 inColor;

layout(location = 0) out vec3 fragColor;

void main() {

gl_Position = vec4(inPosition, 0.0, 1.0);

fragColor = inColor;

}
```

And a corresponding fragment shader:

```glsl
#version 450

layout(location = 0) in vec3 fragColor;

layout(location = 0) out vec4 outColor;

void main() {

outColor = vec4(fragColor, 1.0);

}
```

Compiling Shaders to SPIR-V

Shaders need to be compiled to SPIR-V before they can be used in Vulkan. This can be done using the glslangValidator tool:

glslangValidator -V shader.vert

glslangValidator -V shader.frag

Integrating Shaders into the Pipeline

After compiling the shaders to SPIR-V and creating shader modules, they can be integrated into the pipeline. This involves setting up the VkPipelineShaderStageCreateInfo structures and including them in the pipeline creation process.

```cpp
VkPipelineShaderStageCreateInfo shaderStages[] = {vertShaderStageInfo, fragShaderStageInfo};

VkGraphicsPipelineCreateInfo pipelineInfo = {};

pipelineInfo.sType = VK_STRUCTURE_TYPE_GRAPHICS_PIPELINE_CREATE_INFO;

pipelineInfo.stageCount = 2;

pipelineInfo.pStages = shaderStages;

// Other pipeline configurations...

if (vkCreateGraphicsPipelines(device, VK_NULL_HANDLE, 1, &pipelineInfo, nullptr, &graphicsPipeline) != VK_SUCCESS) {

throw std::runtime_error("failed to create graphics pipeline!");

}
```

By understanding shaders and shader modules in Vulkan, developers can harness the full power of the GPU to implement advanced rendering techniques. Shaders offer the flexibility to customize every stage of the graphics pipeline, enabling a wide range of visual effects and optimizations.

Fixed-Function Stages

In addition to programmable shader stages, the Vulkan pipeline includes several fixed-function stages. These stages perform specific operations that do not involve custom shaders but can be configured to achieve the desired rendering outcomes. Understanding and configuring these stages is essential for efficient rendering in Vulkan.

Input Assembly

The input assembly stage assembles vertex data into geometric primitives such as points, lines, and triangles. This stage is configured using VkPipelineInputAssemblyStateCreateInfo.

```
VkPipelineInputAssemblyStateCreateInfo inputAssembly = {};

inputAssembly.sType                                    =
VK_STRUCTURE_TYPE_PIPELINE_INPUT_ASSEMBLY_STATE

inputAssembly.topology                                 =
VK_PRIMITIVE_TOPOLOGY_TRIANGLE_LIST;

inputAssembly.primitiveRestartEnable = VK_FALSE;
```

Rasterization

The rasterization stage converts geometric primitives into fragments. This stage involves several sub-stages, including viewport transformation, clipping, and culling. The configuration is done using VkPipelineRasterizationStateCreateInfo.

```
VkPipelineRasterizationStateCreateInfo rasterizer = {};

rasterizer.sType                                        =
VK_STRUCTURE_TYPE_PIPELINE_RASTERIZATION_STATE_CRE

rasterizer.depthClampEnable = VK_FALSE;

rasterizer.rasterizerDiscardEnable = VK_FALSE;

rasterizer.polygonMode = VK_POLYGON_MODE_FILL;

rasterizer.lineWidth = 1.0f;

rasterizer.cullMode = VK_CULL_MODE_BACK_BIT;

rasterizer.frontFace = VK_FRONT_FACE_CLOCKWISE;

rasterizer.depthBiasEnable = VK_FALSE;
```

Multisampling

Multisampling is used for anti-aliasing, which smooths out jagged edges in rendered images. The multisample stage is configured using VkPipelineMultisampleStateCreateInfo.

```
VkPipelineMultisampleStateCreateInfo multisampling = {};

multisampling.sType                                     =
VK_STRUCTURE_TYPE_PIPELINE_MULTISAMPLE_STATE_CREA

multisampling.sampleShadingEnable = VK_FALSE;

multisampling.rasterizationSamples                      =
VK_SAMPLE_COUNT_1_BIT;
```

Depth and Stencil Testing

Depth and stencil testing are crucial for rendering scenes with proper depth and occlusion. These tests are configured using VkPipelineDepthStencilStateCreateInfo.

```
VkPipelineDepthStencilStateCreateInfo depthStencil = {};

depthStencil.sType                                          = VK_STRUCTURE_TYPE_PIPELINE_DEPTH_STENCIL_STATE_C

depthStencil.depthTestEnable = VK_TRUE;

depthStencil.depthWriteEnable = VK_TRUE;

depthStencil.depthCompareOp = VK_COMPARE_OP_LESS;

depthStencil.depthBoundsTestEnable = VK_FALSE;

depthStencil.stencilTestEnable = VK_FALSE;
```

Color Blending

Color blending determines how the colors of fragments are combined with the colors already present in the framebuffer. This stage is configured using VkPipelineColorBlendStateCreateInfo and VkPipelineColorBlendAttachmentState.

```
VkPipelineColorBlendAttachmentState colorBlendAttachment = {};

colorBlendAttachment.colorWriteMask                         =
VK_COLOR_COMPONENT_R_BIT                                     |
VK_COLOR_COMPONENT_G_BIT                                     |
VK_COLOR_COMPONENT_B_BIT                                     |
VK_COLOR_COMPONENT_A_BIT;

colorBlendAttachment.blendEnable = VK_FALSE;
```

```cpp
VkPipelineColorBlendStateCreateInfo colorBlending = {};

colorBlending.sType                                    =
VK_STRUCTURE_TYPE_PIPELINE_COLOR_BLEND_STATE_CREA

colorBlending.logicOpEnable = VK_FALSE;

colorBlending.logicOp = VK_LOGIC_OP_COPY;

colorBlending.attachmentCount = 1;

colorBlending.pAttachments = &colorBlendAttachment;

colorBlending.blendConstants[0] = 0.0f;

colorBlending.blendConstants[1] = 0.0f;

colorBlending.blendConstants[2] = 0.0f;

colorBlending.blendConstants[3] = 0.0f;
```

Configuring Fixed-Function Stages

Configuring the fixed-function stages involves setting up the corresponding structures and including them in the pipeline creation process. This ensures that the pipeline operates correctly and efficiently.

```cpp
VkGraphicsPipelineCreateInfo pipelineInfo = {};

pipelineInfo.sType                                    =
VK_STRUCTURE_TYPE_GRAPHICS_PIPELINE_CREATE_INFO;

pipelineInfo.stageCount = 2;

pipelineInfo.pStages = shaderStages;

pipelineInfo.pVertexInputState = &vertexInputInfo;

pipelineInfo.pInputAssemblyState = &inputAssembly;
```

```
pipelineInfo.pViewportState = &viewportState;

pipelineInfo.pRasterizationState = &rasterizer;

pipelineInfo.pMultisampleState = &multisampling;

pipelineInfo.pDepthStencilState = &depthStencil;

pipelineInfo.pColorBlendState = &colorBlending;

pipelineInfo.layout = pipelineLayout;

pipelineInfo.renderPass = renderPass;

pipelineInfo.subpass = 0;

if (vkCreateGraphicsPipelines(device, VK_NULL_HANDLE, 1,
&pipelineInfo, nullptr, &graphicsPipeline) != VK_SUCCESS) {

throw std::runtime_error("failed to create graphics pipeline!");

}
```

By understanding and configuring the fixed-function stages, developers can leverage Vulkan's powerful capabilities to create efficient and visually stunning graphics applications. These stages provide essential functionality and complement the programmable shader stages, resulting in a comprehensive and flexible rendering pipeline.

Chapter 4: Drawing Geometry

Vertex Input and Attributes

In Vulkan, drawing geometry begins with defining how vertex data is provided to the graphics pipeline. This involves specifying the format and structure of vertex data, and creating buffers to hold this data. The vertex input stage is responsible for processing this data and making it available to subsequent pipeline stages.

To set up vertex input, you need to define a VkVertexInputBindingDescription, which describes the rate at which data is loaded from memory. This structure includes the following fields:

- binding: the binding number that this structure binds to. This corresponds to the binding used in the vertex shader.

- stride: the byte offset between consecutive vertex attributes.

- inputRate: whether vertex data is per-vertex or per-instance.

Here is an example of setting up a binding description for vertex input:

```
VkVertexInputBindingDescription bindingDescription = {};

bindingDescription.binding = 0;

bindingDescription.stride = sizeof(Vertex);

bindingDescription.inputRate = VK_VERTEX_INPUT_RATE_VERTEX;
```

Next, you define VkVertexInputAttributeDescription structures, which describe the format and location of each vertex attribute. Each attribute description includes:

- location: the location of the attribute in the shader.

- binding: the binding number that this attribute is bound to.

- format: the data type and size of the attribute.

- offset: the byte offset of the attribute within each vertex.

Here's an example of defining attribute descriptions for a vertex structure containing position and color attributes:

```cpp
std::array<VkVertexInputAttributeDescription, 2> attributeDescriptions = {};

attributeDescriptions[0].location = 0;

attributeDescriptions[0].binding = 0;

attributeDescriptions[0].format = VK_FORMAT_R32G32B32_SFLOAT;

attributeDescriptions[0].offset = offsetof(Vertex, pos);

attributeDescriptions[1].location = 1;

attributeDescriptions[1].binding = 0;

attributeDescriptions[1].format = VK_FORMAT_R32G32B32A32_SFLOAT;

attributeDescriptions[1].offset = offsetof(Vertex, color);
```

Once you have defined the binding and attribute descriptions, you need to create a VkPipelineVertexInputStateCreateInfo structure that includes them:

```cpp
VkPipelineVertexInputStateCreateInfo vertexInputInfo = {};

vertexInputInfo.sType                                         =
VK_STRUCTURE_TYPE_PIPELINE_VERTEX_INPUT_STATE_CRE/

vertexInputInfo.vertexBindingDescriptionCount                =
static_cast<uint32_t>(bindingDescriptions.size());

vertexInputInfo.pVertexBindingDescriptions                   =
bindingDescriptions.data();

vertexInputInfo.vertexAttributeDescriptionCount              =
static_cast<uint32_t>(attributeDescriptions.size());

vertexInputInfo.pVertexAttributeDescriptions                 =
attributeDescriptions.data();
```

With the vertex input state defined, you can proceed to create a vertex buffer. A vertex buffer is a special type of buffer that holds vertex data. To create a vertex buffer, you need to allocate memory and upload the vertex data to this memory.

First, create a buffer with vkCreateBuffer:

```cpp
VkBufferCreateInfo bufferInfo = {};

bufferInfo.sType                                             =
VK_STRUCTURE_TYPE_BUFFER_CREATE_INFO;

bufferInfo.size = bufferSize;

bufferInfo.usage                                            =
VK_BUFFER_USAGE_VERTEX_BUFFER_BIT;
```

```cpp
bufferInfo.sharingMode = VK_SHARING_MODE_EXCLUSIVE;

VkBuffer vertexBuffer;

if (vkCreateBuffer(device, &bufferInfo, nullptr, &vertexBuffer) !=
VK_SUCCESS) {

throw std::runtime_error("failed to create vertex buffer!");

}
```

Next, allocate memory for the buffer and bind it:

```cpp
VkMemoryRequirements memRequirements;

vkGetBufferMemoryRequirements(device,                vertexBuffer,
&memRequirements);

VkMemoryAllocateInfo allocInfo = {};

allocInfo.sType                                                    =
VK_STRUCTURE_TYPE_MEMORY_ALLOCATE_INFO;

allocInfo.allocationSize = memRequirements.size;

allocInfo.memoryTypeIndex                                          =
findMemoryType(memRequirements.memoryTypeBits,
VK_MEMORY_PROPERTY_HOST_VISIBLE_BIT                                 |
VK_MEMORY_PROPERTY_HOST_COHERENT_BIT);

VkDeviceMemory vertexBufferMemory;

if       (vkAllocateMemory(device,         &allocInfo,        nullptr,
&vertexBufferMemory) != VK_SUCCESS) {

throw std::runtime_error("failed to allocate vertex buffer memory!");

}
```

vkBindBufferMemory(device, vertexBuffer, vertexBufferMemory, 0);

Finally, map the memory and copy the vertex data to the buffer:

void* data;

vkMapMemory(device, vertexBufferMemory, 0, bufferSize, 0, &data);

memcpy(data, vertices.data(), (size_t)bufferSize);

vkUnmapMemory(device, vertexBufferMemory);

This process sets up the vertex input stage, ensuring that the vertex data is correctly formatted and available to the pipeline for rendering.

Index Buffers

In addition to vertex buffers, Vulkan uses index buffers to optimize rendering by reusing vertices. An index buffer holds indices that reference vertices in a vertex buffer, allowing the GPU to draw complex shapes efficiently.

To create an index buffer, follow a process similar to creating a vertex buffer. Start by defining the indices and creating a buffer with vkCreateBuffer:

std::vector<uint16_t> indices = {0, 1, 2, 2, 3, 0};

VkBufferCreateInfo bufferInfo = {};

bufferInfo.sType   = VK_STRUCTURE_TYPE_BUFFER_CREATE_INFO;

bufferInfo.size = sizeof(indices[0]) * indices.size();

bufferInfo.usage = VK_BUFFER_USAGE_INDEX_BUFFER_BIT;

```cpp
bufferInfo.sharingMode = VK_SHARING_MODE_EXCLUSIVE;

VkBuffer indexBuffer;

if (vkCreateBuffer(device, &bufferInfo, nullptr, &indexBuffer) != VK_SUCCESS) {

throw std::runtime_error("failed to create index buffer!");

}
```

Next, allocate memory for the index buffer and bind it:

```cpp
VkMemoryRequirements memRequirements;

vkGetBufferMemoryRequirements(device, indexBuffer, &memRequirements);

VkMemoryAllocateInfo allocInfo = {};

allocInfo.sType = VK_STRUCTURE_TYPE_MEMORY_ALLOCATE_INFO;

allocInfo.allocationSize = memRequirements.size;

allocInfo.memoryTypeIndex = findMemoryType(memRequirements.memoryTypeBits, VK_MEMORY_PROPERTY_HOST_VISIBLE_BIT | VK_MEMORY_PROPERTY_HOST_COHERENT_BIT);

VkDeviceMemory indexBufferMemory;

if (vkAllocateMemory(device, &allocInfo, nullptr, &indexBufferMemory) != VK_SUCCESS) {

throw std::runtime_error("failed to allocate index buffer memory!");

}
```

```
vkBindBufferMemory(device, indexBuffer, indexBufferMemory, 0);
```

Map the memory and copy the index data to the buffer:

```
void* data;

vkMapMemory(device, indexBufferMemory, 0, bufferInfo.size, 0,
&data);

memcpy(data, indices.data(), (size_t)bufferInfo.size);

vkUnmapMemory(device, indexBufferMemory);
```

With the index buffer created and populated, you can bind it during the drawing process. Binding the index buffer is done using the vkCmdBindIndexBuffer command:

```
vkCmdBindIndexBuffer(commandBuffer, indexBuffer, 0,
VK_INDEX_TYPE_UINT16);
```

During the drawing command, specify the use of indices:

```
vkCmdDrawIndexed(commandBuffer,
static_cast<uint32_t>(indices.size()), 1, 0, 0, 0);
```

Using index buffers allows for more efficient rendering, as it reduces the amount of vertex data that needs to be processed and transferred.

Command Buffers and Command Pools

Command buffers in Vulkan are used to record rendering commands that the GPU will execute. They are allocated from command pools, which manage the memory used by command buffers.

To create a command pool, use the vkCreateCommandPool function. Command pools are created with specific queue families in mind, so you need to specify the queue family index:

```cpp
VkCommandPoolCreateInfo poolInfo = {};

poolInfo.sType = VK_STRUCTURE_TYPE_COMMAND_POOL_CREATE_INFO;

poolInfo.queueFamilyIndex = graphicsQueueFamilyIndex;

poolInfo.flags = 0; // Optional

VkCommandPool commandPool;

if (vkCreateCommandPool(device, &poolInfo, nullptr, &commandPool) != VK_SUCCESS) {

throw std::runtime_error("failed to create command pool!");

}
```

Once you have a command pool, you can allocate command buffers from it. Command buffers can be primary or secondary. Primary command buffers can be submitted to a queue for execution, while secondary command buffers can only be called from primary command buffers.

Here's an example of allocating primary command buffers:

```cpp
VkCommandBufferAllocateInfo allocInfo = {};

allocInfo.sType = VK_STRUCTURE_TYPE_COMMAND_BUFFER_ALLOCATE_IN

allocInfo.commandPool = commandPool;

allocInfo.level = VK_COMMAND_BUFFER_LEVEL_PRIMARY;

allocInfo.commandBufferCount = 1;

VkCommandBuffer commandBuffer;
```

```cpp
if            (vkAllocateCommandBuffers(device,            &allocInfo,
&commandBuffer) != VK_SUCCESS) {

throw std::runtime_error("failed to allocate command buffers!");

}
```

To record commands into a command buffer, begin by calling vkBeginCommandBuffer:

```cpp
VkCommandBufferBeginInfo beginInfo = {};

beginInfo.sType                                                    =
VK_STRUCTURE_TYPE_COMMAND_BUFFER_BEGIN_INFO;

beginInfo.flags                                                    =
VK_COMMAND_BUFFER_USAGE_SIMULTANEOUS_USE_BIT;
// Optional

beginInfo.pInheritanceInfo = nullptr; // Optional

if   (vkBeginCommandBuffer(commandBuffer,   &beginInfo)   !=
VK_SUCCESS) {

throw std::runtime_error("failed to begin recording command
buffer!");

}
```

Record commands such as binding the pipeline, setting viewport and scissor states, binding vertex and index buffers, and drawing:

```cpp
vkCmdBindPipeline(commandBuffer,
VK_PIPELINE_BIND_POINT_GRAPHICS, graphicsPipeline);

VkBuffer vertexBuffers[] = {vertexBuffer};

VkDeviceSize offsets[] = {0};
```

```
vkCmdBindVertexBuffers(commandBuffer, 0, 1, vertexBuffers,
offsets);

vkCmdBindIndexBuffer(commandBuffer, indexBuffer, 0,
VK_INDEX_TYPE_UINT16);

vkCmdDrawIndexed(commandBuffer,
static_cast<uint32_t>(indices.size()), 1, 0, 0, 0);
```

Finally, end the command buffer recording with vkEndCommandBuffer:

```
if (vkEndCommandBuffer(commandBuffer) != VK_SUCCESS) {

throw std::runtime_error("failed to record command buffer!");

}
```

Command buffers are submitted to a queue for execution using vkQueueSubmit. You can create synchronization objects such as fences to ensure that the CPU waits for the GPU to complete command buffer execution:

```
VkSubmitInfo submitInfo = {};

submitInfo.sType = VK_STRUCTURE_TYPE_SUBMIT_INFO;

submitInfo.commandBufferCount = 1;

submitInfo.pCommandBuffers = &commandBuffer;

VkFenceCreateInfo fenceInfo = {};

fenceInfo.sType = VK_STRUCTURE_TYPE_FENCE_CREATE_INFO;

VkFence fence;
```

```cpp
if (vkCreateFence(device, &fenceInfo, nullptr, &fence) !=
VK_SUCCESS) {

throw std::runtime_error("failed to create fence!");

}

if (vkQueueSubmit(graphicsQueue, 1, &submitInfo, fence) !=
VK_SUCCESS) {

throw std::runtime_error("failed to submit draw command buffer!");

}

vkWaitForFences(device, 1, &fence, VK_TRUE, UINT64_MAX);
```

By recording commands in command buffers and submitting them to
the GPU, you achieve efficient and flexible rendering in Vulkan.

Chapter 5: Memory Management

Memory Allocation and Management

Efficient memory allocation and management are critical for achieving high performance in Vulkan applications. Vulkan provides a low-level, explicit control over memory, allowing developers to optimize resource usage tailored to their application's specific needs.

To allocate memory in Vulkan, you first need to determine the memory requirements for your buffers or images. This involves querying the memory requirements using vkGetBufferMemoryRequirements or vkGetImageMemoryRequirements. These functions provide information about the size, alignment, and memory type bits, which you can use to find a suitable memory type.

VkMemoryRequirements memRequirements;

vkGetBufferMemoryRequirements(device, buffer, &memRequirements);

Next, you need to choose a memory type that is suitable for your resource. This involves examining the memory type bits and selecting a type that matches your requirements. The VkPhysicalDeviceMemoryProperties structure contains information about the available memory types and heaps on the physical device.

VkPhysicalDeviceMemoryProperties memProperties;

vkGetPhysicalDeviceMemoryProperties(physicalDevice, &memProperties);

uint32_t memoryTypeIndex = findMemoryType(memRequirements.memoryTypeBits,

```
VK_MEMORY_PROPERTY_HOST_VISIBLE_BIT |

VK_MEMORY_PROPERTY_HOST_COHERENT_BIT);
```

The findMemoryType function is a utility that helps find an appropriate memory type index based on the requirements and properties.

```cpp
uint32_t              findMemoryType(uint32_t              typeFilter,
VkMemoryPropertyFlags properties) {

for (uint32_t i = 0; i < memProperties.memoryTypeCount; i++) {

if       ((typeFilter       &       (1       <<       i))       &&
(memProperties.memoryTypes[i].propertyFlags  &  properties)  ==
properties) {

return i;

}

}

throw std::runtime_error("failed to find suitable memory type!");

}
```

Once you have determined the appropriate memory type, you can allocate memory using vkAllocateMemory. This function requires a VkMemoryAllocateInfo structure that specifies the allocation size and memory type index.

```cpp
VkMemoryAllocateInfo allocInfo = {};

allocInfo.sType                                               =
VK_STRUCTURE_TYPE_MEMORY_ALLOCATE_INFO;

allocInfo.allocationSize = memRequirements.size;
```

```cpp
allocInfo.memoryTypeIndex = memoryTypeIndex;

VkDeviceMemory bufferMemory;

if (vkAllocateMemory(device, &allocInfo, nullptr, &bufferMemory)
!= VK_SUCCESS) {

throw std::runtime_error("failed to allocate buffer memory!");

}
```

After allocating the memory, you need to bind it to the buffer or image using vkBindBufferMemory or vkBindImageMemory.

```cpp
vkBindBufferMemory(device, buffer, bufferMemory, 0);
```

Managing memory efficiently also involves understanding the different memory properties, such as VK_MEMORY_PROPERTY_HOST_VISIBLE_BIT, VK_MEMORY_PROPERTY_HOST_COHERENT_BIT, and VK_MEMORY_PROPERTY_DEVICE_LOCAL_BIT. These properties determine how the memory can be accessed and optimized for performance.

Memory mapping is another important aspect. To write data to a buffer, you map the memory to a host-accessible pointer using vkMapMemory, perform the data transfer, and then unmap the memory using vkUnmapMemory.

```cpp
void* data;

vkMapMemory(device, bufferMemory, 0, bufferSize, 0, &data);

memcpy(data, bufferData, (size_t) bufferSize);

vkUnmapMemory(device, bufferMemory);
```

Memory management in Vulkan also requires synchronization to ensure that memory operations are completed before they are accessed by the GPU. This involves using fences, semaphores, and events to coordinate memory usage.

Finally, cleaning up resources is crucial to avoid memory leaks. Always free allocated memory using vkFreeMemory when it is no longer needed.

```
vkFreeMemory(device, bufferMemory, nullptr);
```

Proper memory allocation and management strategies can significantly impact the performance and efficiency of Vulkan applications. Understanding and leveraging Vulkan's memory management capabilities allows developers to create high-performance graphics and compute applications.

Buffer and Image Management

Buffers and images are fundamental to Vulkan applications, representing memory allocated for vertex data, textures, and other resources. Managing these resources efficiently is key to maximizing performance and resource utilization.

Buffers in Vulkan are used to store a variety of data types, such as vertex attributes, index data, and uniform data. Creating a buffer involves specifying its size and usage flags in a VkBufferCreateInfo structure, then creating the buffer using vkCreateBuffer.

```
VkBufferCreateInfo bufferInfo = {};

bufferInfo.sType                                    =
VK_STRUCTURE_TYPE_BUFFER_CREATE_INFO;

bufferInfo.size = bufferSize;
```

```
bufferInfo.usage = VK_BUFFER_USAGE_VERTEX_BUFFER_BIT;

bufferInfo.sharingMode = VK_SHARING_MODE_EXCLUSIVE;

VkBuffer vertexBuffer;

if (vkCreateBuffer(device, &bufferInfo, nullptr, &vertexBuffer) != VK_SUCCESS) {

throw std::runtime_error("failed to create vertex buffer!");

}
```

After creating the buffer, you need to allocate memory for it and bind the memory to the buffer. This involves querying the memory requirements, finding a suitable memory type, allocating memory, and binding it to the buffer.

Images in Vulkan are used for textures, render targets, and other image-based resources. Creating an image involves specifying its type, format, extent, and usage flags in a VkImageCreateInfo structure, then creating the image using vkCreateImage.

```
VkImageCreateInfo imageInfo = {};

imageInfo.sType = VK_STRUCTURE_TYPE_IMAGE_CREATE_INFO;

imageInfo.imageType = VK_IMAGE_TYPE_2D;

imageInfo.extent.width = texWidth;

imageInfo.extent.height = texHeight;

imageInfo.extent.depth = 1;

imageInfo.mipLevels = 1;
```

```
imageInfo.arrayLayers = 1;

imageInfo.format = VK_FORMAT_R8G8B8A8_SRGB;

imageInfo.tiling = VK_IMAGE_TILING_OPTIMAL;

imageInfo.initialLayout = VK_IMAGE_LAYOUT_UNDEFINED;

imageInfo.usage = VK_IMAGE_USAGE_TRANSFER_DST_BIT |
VK_IMAGE_USAGE_SAMPLED_BIT;

imageInfo.samples = VK_SAMPLE_COUNT_1_BIT;

imageInfo.sharingMode = VK_SHARING_MODE_EXCLUSIVE;

VkImage textureImage;

if (vkCreateImage(device, &imageInfo, nullptr, &textureImage) !=
VK_SUCCESS) {

throw std::runtime_error("failed to create texture image!");

}
```

Like buffers, images require memory allocation and binding. You query the memory requirements, find a suitable memory type, allocate memory, and bind it to the image.

Managing the layout of images is crucial for performance. Vulkan images can be in different layouts, such as VK_IMAGE_LAYOUT_UNDEFINED, VK_IMAGE_LAYOUT_TRANSFER_DST_OPTIMAL, and VK_IMAGE_LAYOUT_SHADER_READ_ONLY_OPTIMAL. Transitioning between layouts involves using image memory barriers in command buffers.

```cpp
VkCommandBuffer              commandBuffer              =
beginSingleTimeCommands();

VkImageMemoryBarrier barrier = {};

barrier.sType                                           =
VK_STRUCTURE_TYPE_IMAGE_MEMORY_BARRIER;

barrier.oldLayout = VK_IMAGE_LAYOUT_UNDEFINED;

barrier.newLayout                                      =
VK_IMAGE_LAYOUT_TRANSFER_DST_OPTIMAL;

barrier.srcQueueFamilyIndex                            =
VK_QUEUE_FAMILY_IGNORED;

barrier.dstQueueFamilyIndex                            =
VK_QUEUE_FAMILY_IGNORED;

barrier.image = textureImage;

barrier.subresourceRange.aspectMask                    =
VK_IMAGE_ASPECT_COLOR_BIT;

barrier.subresourceRange.baseMipLevel = 0;

barrier.subresourceRange.levelCount = 1;

barrier.subresourceRange.baseArrayLayer = 0;

barrier.subresourceRange.layerCount = 1;

vkCmdPipelineBarrier(

commandBuffer,

VK_PIPELINE_STAGE_TOP_OF_PIPE_BIT,
VK_PIPELINE_STAGE_TRANSFER_BIT,
```

```
0,

0, nullptr,

0, nullptr,

1, &barrier

);
```

endSingleTimeCommands(commandBuffer);

Efficiently managing buffers and images includes minimizing memory fragmentation, optimizing memory usage patterns, and ensuring proper synchronization. Using tools like Vulkan Memory Allocator (VMA) can simplify memory management by providing higher-level abstractions and optimizations.

Proper buffer and image management ensures that your Vulkan application can handle complex scenes and large datasets while maintaining high performance and stability.

Synchronization Primitives

Synchronization is a critical aspect of Vulkan programming, ensuring that operations occur in the correct order and that resources are accessed safely by multiple threads or the GPU. Vulkan provides several synchronization primitives, including fences, semaphores, and events, each serving different purposes.

Fences are used to synchronize operations between the CPU and the GPU. A fence is a binary signal that can be set or reset. When you submit a command buffer for execution, you can associate a fence with the submission. The fence will be signaled when the GPU has completed the execution of the command buffer. You can then use the fence to wait for the completion on the CPU side.

```cpp
VkFenceCreateInfo fenceInfo = {};

fenceInfo.sType =
VK_STRUCTURE_TYPE_FENCE_CREATE_INFO;

VkFence fence;

if (vkCreateFence(device, &fenceInfo, nullptr, &fence) !=
VK_SUCCESS) {

throw std::runtime_error("failed to create fence!");

}

// Submit command buffer with fence

VkSubmitInfo submitInfo = {};

submitInfo.sType = VK_STRUCTURE_TYPE_SUBMIT_INFO;

submitInfo.commandBufferCount = 1;

submitInfo.pCommandBuffers = &commandBuffer;

if (vkQueueSubmit(graphicsQueue, 1, &submitInfo, fence) !=
VK_SUCCESS) {

throw std::runtime_error("failed to submit draw command buffer!");

}

// Wait for the fence to be signaled

vkWaitForFences(device, 1, &fence, VK_TRUE, UINT64_MAX);
```

Semaphores are used to synchronize operations within or between command queues. They are used to signal the completion of an operation in one command buffer so that another command buffer can start executing. For example, you can use semaphores to synchronize the rendering and presentation stages.

```cpp
VkSemaphoreCreateInfo semaphoreInfo = {};

semaphoreInfo.sType                                    =
VK_STRUCTURE_TYPE_SEMAPHORE_CREATE_INFO;

VkSemaphore imageAvailableSemaphore;

VkSemaphore renderFinishedSemaphore;

if     (vkCreateSemaphore(device,        &semaphoreInfo,        nullptr,
&imageAvailableSemaphore) != VK_SUCCESS ||

vkCreateSemaphore(device,            &semaphoreInfo,           nullptr,
&renderFinishedSemaphore) != VK_SUCCESS) {

throw std::runtime_error("failed to create semaphores!");

}

// Wait for the image to be available for rendering

VkSubmitInfo submitInfo = {};

submitInfo.sType = VK_STRUCTURE_TYPE_SUBMIT_INFO;

VkSemaphore waitSemaphores[] = {imageAvailableSemaphore};

VkPipelineStageFlags               waitStages[]               =
{VK_PIPELINE_STAGE_COLOR_ATTACHMENT_OUTPUT_BIT};

submitInfo.waitSemaphoreCount = 1;

submitInfo.pWaitSemaphores = waitSemaphores;

submitInfo.pWaitDstStageMask = waitStages;
```

```cpp
// Signal that rendering is finished

VkSemaphore signalSemaphores[] = {renderFinishedSemaphore};

submitInfo.signalSemaphoreCount = 1;

submitInfo.pSignalSemaphores = signalSemaphores;

if (vkQueueSubmit(graphicsQueue, 1, &submitInfo, VK_NULL_HANDLE) != VK_SUCCESS) {

throw std::runtime_error("failed to submit draw command buffer!");

}
```

Events are used for finer-grained synchronization within command buffers. They can be set or reset at specific points in a command buffer, allowing you to synchronize operations without submitting the command buffer multiple times.

```cpp
VkEventCreateInfo eventInfo = {};

eventInfo.sType = VK_STRUCTURE_TYPE_EVENT_CREATE_INFO;

VkEvent event;

if (vkCreateEvent(device, &eventInfo, nullptr, &event) != VK_SUCCESS) {

throw std::runtime_error("failed to create event!");

}

// Set the event at a specific point in the command buffer

vkCmdSetEvent(commandBuffer, event, VK_PIPELINE_STAGE_VERTEX_SHADER_BIT);
```

```
// Wait for the event in another command buffer

vkCmdWaitEvents(commandBuffer,                    1,                  &event,
VK_PIPELINE_STAGE_VERTEX_SHADER_BIT,
VK_PIPELINE_STAGE_FRAGMENT_SHADER_BIT,

0, nullptr, 0, nullptr, 0, nullptr);
```

Understanding and using these synchronization primitives correctly is essential for developing efficient and stable Vulkan applications. Proper synchronization ensures that resources are accessed safely and that operations occur in the intended order, preventing data corruption and undefined behavior.

By leveraging fences, semaphores, and events, you can optimize the execution flow of your Vulkan application, ensuring that the CPU and GPU work together seamlessly and efficiently.

Chapter 6: Advanced Rendering Techniques

Depth and Stencil Testing

Depth and stencil testing are fundamental techniques in 3D rendering that control the visibility of objects in a scene. They are used to manage how pixels are written to the framebuffer based on their depth values and stencil operations.

Depth testing ensures that pixels closer to the camera overwrite those farther away, creating a correct perception of depth. To enable depth testing in Vulkan, you need to set up a depth buffer and configure the depth stencil state in the pipeline.

```cpp
VkPipelineDepthStencilStateCreateInfo depthStencilInfo{};

depthStencilInfo.sType                                          = VK_STRUCTURE_TYPE_PIPELINE_DEPTH_STENCIL_STATE_C

depthStencilInfo.depthTestEnable = VK_TRUE;

depthStencilInfo.depthWriteEnable = VK_TRUE;

depthStencilInfo.depthCompareOp = VK_COMPARE_OP_LESS;

depthStencilInfo.depthBoundsTestEnable = VK_FALSE;

depthStencilInfo.minDepthBounds = 0.0f;

depthStencilInfo.maxDepthBounds = 1.0f;

depthStencilInfo.stencilTestEnable = VK_FALSE;
```

In the above code, depthTestEnable and depthWriteEnable are set to VK_TRUE to enable depth testing and writing. The depth comparison operation is set to VK_COMPARE_OP_LESS, meaning that fragments with a depth less than the current depth buffer value will pass the depth test.

Stencil testing provides additional control over pixel rendering using stencil buffer operations. It allows masking certain parts of the screen, implementing effects like shadows, outlines, or mirrors. The stencil buffer stores integer values that are updated based on stencil operations.

Configuring stencil operations involves setting up the stencil test in the VkPipelineDepthStencilStateCreateInfo structure. The stencil test can be customized to perform different actions based on the comparison of stencil values.

```
VkStencilOpState stencilOp{};

stencilOp.failOp = VK_STENCIL_OP_KEEP;

stencilOp.passOp = VK_STENCIL_OP_REPLACE;

stencilOp.depthFailOp = VK_STENCIL_OP_KEEP;

stencilOp.compareOp = VK_COMPARE_OP_ALWAYS;

stencilOp.compareMask = 0xFF;

stencilOp.writeMask = 0xFF;

stencilOp.reference = 1;
```

In this code, failOp specifies what happens if the stencil test fails, passOp specifies the action when the stencil test passes, and depthFailOp specifies the action if the depth test fails but the stencil test passes. The compareOp determines the comparison operation, and compareMask, writeMask, and reference are used to control the stencil test's behavior.

Combining depth and stencil testing can achieve complex rendering techniques, such as shadow volumes, where the stencil buffer is used to create shadows by incrementing and decrementing stencil values.

Implementing depth and stencil testing requires careful management of the depth and stencil states in your Vulkan application. It involves configuring the pipeline, creating appropriate buffers, and ensuring correct operations during rendering.

Depth and stencil testing are powerful tools that provide fine-grained control over pixel rendering, enabling advanced visual effects and accurate scene representation.

Multisampling

Multisampling is a technique used to improve the visual quality of rendered images by reducing aliasing, which appears as jagged edges on objects. In Vulkan, multisampling is achieved by sampling a pixel multiple times at different sample points and averaging the results.

To enable multisampling, you need to configure the multisampling state in your pipeline. This involves specifying the number of samples per pixel and setting up the appropriate structures.

```
VkPipelineMultisampleStateCreateInfo multisampling{};

multisampling.sType                                    =
VK_STRUCTURE_TYPE_PIPELINE_MULTISAMPLE_STATE_CR

multisampling.sampleShadingEnable = VK_TRUE;

multisampling.rasterizationSamples                     =
VK_SAMPLE_COUNT_4_BIT;
```

multisampling.minSampleShading = .2f;

multisampling.pSampleMask = nullptr;

multisampling.alphaToCoverageEnable = VK_FALSE;

multisampling.alphaToOneEnable = VK_FALSE;

In this example, rasterizationSamples is set to VK_SAMPLE_COUNT_4_BIT, meaning each pixel will be sampled four times. The sampleShadingEnable flag enables sample shading, and minSampleShading specifies the minimum fraction of sample shading.

The multisampling configuration must be compatible with the render pass and framebuffer. This involves ensuring that the attachments in the render pass support the desired sample count.

VkAttachmentDescription colorAttachment{};

colorAttachment.format = swapChainImageFormat;

colorAttachment.samples = VK_SAMPLE_COUNT_4_BIT;

colorAttachment.loadOp = VK_ATTACHMENT_LOAD_OP_CLEAR;

colorAttachment.storeOp = VK_ATTACHMENT_STORE_OP_STORE;

colorAttachment.stencilLoadOp = VK_ATTACHMENT_LOAD_OP_DONT_CARE;

colorAttachment.stencilStoreOp = VK_ATTACHMENT_STORE_OP_DONT_CARE;

colorAttachment.initialLayout = VK_IMAGE_LAYOUT_UNDEFINED;

```
colorAttachment.finalLayout                              =
VK_IMAGE_LAYOUT_PRESENT_SRC_KHR;
```

In this code, the samples field of the color attachment description is set to VK_SAMPLE_COUNT_4_BIT to match the multisampling configuration.

Multisampling can significantly improve image quality, but it also increases the computational workload and memory usage. Therefore, it is essential to balance the quality improvement with performance considerations.

To use multisampling effectively, you need to understand the trade-offs involved and configure your Vulkan application accordingly. This includes selecting appropriate sample counts, managing memory and computational resources, and optimizing your pipeline configuration.

By leveraging multisampling, you can achieve smoother edges and higher visual fidelity in your Vulkan applications, enhancing the overall rendering quality.

Descriptor Sets and Layouts

Descriptor sets and layouts are crucial components in Vulkan for managing resources such as textures, buffers, and samplers. They allow you to bind resources to the pipeline, enabling the shaders to access them during rendering.

A descriptor set layout defines the types and number of resources that can be bound to a pipeline. It is created using the VkDescriptorSetLayoutCreateInfo structure, specifying the bindings and their types.

```
VkDescriptorSetLayoutBinding uboLayoutBinding{};
```

```cpp
uboLayoutBinding.binding = 0;

uboLayoutBinding.descriptorType                        =
VK_DESCRIPTOR_TYPE_UNIFORM_BUFFER;

uboLayoutBinding.descriptorCount = 1;

uboLayoutBinding.stageFlags                            =
VK_SHADER_STAGE_VERTEX_BIT;

uboLayoutBinding.pImmutableSamplers = nullptr;

VkDescriptorSetLayoutCreateInfo layoutInfo{};

layoutInfo.sType                                       =
VK_STRUCTURE_TYPE_DESCRIPTOR_SET_LAYOUT_CREATE_I

layoutInfo.bindingCount = 1;

layoutInfo.pBindings = &uboLayoutBinding;

VkDescriptorSetLayout descriptorSetLayout;

if   (vkCreateDescriptorSetLayout(device,   &layoutInfo,   nullptr,
&descriptorSetLayout) != VK_SUCCESS) {

throw std::runtime_error("failed to create descriptor set layout!");

}
```

In this example, a descriptor set layout is created with a single binding for a uniform buffer accessible in the vertex shader.

Once the descriptor set layout is defined, you can create descriptor sets using the VkDescriptorSetAllocateInfo structure. Descriptor sets are allocated from a descriptor pool, which must be created beforehand.

```cpp
VkDescriptorPoolSize poolSize{};
```

```
poolSize.type                                              =
VK_DESCRIPTOR_TYPE_UNIFORM_BUFFER;

poolSize.descriptorCount                                   =
static_cast<uint32_t>(swapChainImages.size());

VkDescriptorPoolCreateInfo poolInfo{};

poolInfo.sType                                             =
VK_STRUCTURE_TYPE_DESCRIPTOR_POOL_CREATE_INFO;

poolInfo.poolSizeCount = 1;

poolInfo.pPoolSizes = &poolSize;

poolInfo.maxSets = static_cast<uint32_t>(swapChainImages.size());

VkDescriptorPool descriptorPool;

if    (vkCreateDescriptorPool(device,    &poolInfo,    nullptr,
&descriptorPool) != VK_SUCCESS) {

throw std::runtime_error("failed to create descriptor pool!");

}
```

In this code, a descriptor pool is created to allocate uniform buffer descriptors for each swap chain image.

After allocating descriptor sets, you need to update them with the actual resource bindings using the VkWriteDescriptorSet structure.

```
VkDescriptorBufferInfo bufferInfo{};

bufferInfo.buffer = uniformBuffers[i];

bufferInfo.offset = 0;
```

```cpp
bufferInfo.range = sizeof(UniformBufferObject);

VkWriteDescriptorSet descriptorWrite{};

descriptorWrite.sType                                          =
VK_STRUCTURE_TYPE_WRITE_DESCRIPTOR_SET;

descriptorWrite.dstSet = descriptorSets[i];

descriptorWrite.dstBinding = 0;

descriptorWrite.dstArrayElement = 0;

descriptorWrite.descriptorType                                =
VK_DESCRIPTOR_TYPE_UNIFORM_BUFFER;

descriptorWrite.descriptorCount = 1;

descriptorWrite.pBufferInfo = &bufferInfo;

vkUpdateDescriptorSets(device, 1, &descriptorWrite, 0, nullptr);
```

In this code, the descriptor set is updated with the uniform buffer information, allowing the shader to access the buffer during rendering.

Descriptor sets and layouts provide a flexible and efficient way to manage resources in Vulkan. They enable binding resources dynamically, supporting complex rendering techniques and resource management strategies.

Understanding descriptor sets and layouts is essential for developing advanced Vulkan applications. It involves creating and managing layouts, pools, and sets, updating them with resource bindings, and integrating them into the rendering pipeline.

Pipelines with Multiple Subpasses

In Vulkan, subpasses allow you to divide a render pass into multiple stages, enabling more efficient rendering by reusing data within the same render pass. This technique is particularly useful for complex rendering scenarios like deferred shading, where multiple passes are needed to compute the final image.

A subpass in Vulkan is defined within a render pass and can use the attachments declared in the render pass. Subpasses can read from and write to these attachments, facilitating operations like intermediate calculations and post-processing effects.

To create a render pass with multiple subpasses, you first define the subpasses and their dependencies. This involves specifying the attachment references and the order of execution.

VkAttachmentDescription colorAttachment{};

colorAttachment.format = swapChainImageFormat;

colorAttachment.samples = VK_SAMPLE_COUNT_1_BIT;

colorAttachment.loadOp   = VK_ATTACHMENT_LOAD_OP_CLEAR;

colorAttachment.storeOp   = VK_ATTACHMENT_STORE_OP_STORE;

colorAttachment.stencilLoadOp   = VK_ATTACHMENT_LOAD_OP_DONT_CARE;

colorAttachment.stencilStoreOp   = VK_ATTACHMENT_STORE_OP_DONT_CARE;

```cpp
colorAttachment.initialLayout = VK_IMAGE_LAYOUT_UNDEFINED;

colorAttachment.finalLayout = VK_IMAGE_LAYOUT_PRESENT_SRC_KHR;

VkAttachmentReference colorAttachmentRef{};

colorAttachmentRef.attachment = 0;

colorAttachmentRef.layout = VK_IMAGE_LAYOUT_COLOR_ATTACHMENT_OPTIMAL;

VkSubpassDescription subpass1{};

subpass1.pipelineBindPoint = VK_PIPELINE_BIND_POINT_GRAPHICS;

subpass1.colorAttachmentCount = 1;

subpass1.pColorAttachments = &colorAttachmentRef;

VkSubpassDescription subpass2{};

subpass2.pipelineBindPoint = VK_PIPELINE_BIND_POINT_GRAPHICS;

subpass2.colorAttachmentCount = 1;

subpass2.pColorAttachments = &colorAttachmentRef;

subpass2.inputAttachmentCount = 1;

subpass2.pInputAttachments = &colorAttachmentRef;

VkSubpassDependency dependency{};

dependency.srcSubpass = VK_SUBPASS_EXTERNAL;
```

```cpp
dependency.dstSubpass = 0;

dependency.srcStageMask                                   =
VK_PIPELINE_STAGE_COLOR_ATTACHMENT_OUTPUT_BIT

dependency.srcAccessMask = 0;

dependency.dstStageMask                                   =
VK_PIPELINE_STAGE_COLOR_ATTACHMENT_OUTPUT_BIT

dependency.dstAccessMask                                  =
VK_ACCESS_COLOR_ATTACHMENT_WRITE_BIT;

std::array<VkSubpassDescription,  2>  subpasses  =  {subpass1,
subpass2};

std::array<VkSubpassDependency, 1> dependencies = {dependency};

VkRenderPassCreateInfo renderPassInfo{};

renderPassInfo.sType                                      =
VK_STRUCTURE_TYPE_RENDER_PASS_CREATE_INFO;

renderPassInfo.attachmentCount = 1;

renderPassInfo.pAttachments = &colorAttachment;

renderPassInfo.subpassCount                               =
static_cast<uint32_t>(subpasses.size());

renderPassInfo.pSubpasses = subpasses.data();

renderPassInfo.dependencyCount                            =
static_cast<uint32_t>(dependencies.size());

renderPassInfo.pDependencies = dependencies.data();

VkRenderPass renderPass;
```

```
if      (vkCreateRenderPass(device,      &renderPassInfo,      nullptr,
&renderPass) != VK_SUCCESS) {

throw std::runtime_error("failed to create render pass!");

}
```

In this example, two subpasses are defined: one for the initial rendering and another for post-processing. The subpasses share the same color attachment, enabling efficient data reuse.

Using subpasses can optimize rendering performance by minimizing memory bandwidth and synchronization overhead. It allows Vulkan to execute multiple rendering operations within a single render pass, reducing the need for intermediate data transfers and state changes.

However, managing subpasses requires careful planning and understanding of the rendering workflow. You need to define appropriate attachment references, configure subpass dependencies, and ensure correct data flow between subpasses.

By leveraging subpasses, you can implement advanced rendering techniques and optimize your Vulkan applications for better performance and efficiency. This involves designing your render passes with multiple subpasses, configuring dependencies, and integrating them into your rendering pipeline.

Chapter 7: Texture Mapping and Sampling

Image Objects and Image Views

In Vulkan, image objects represent memory allocations that store images (textures) for use in rendering. An image object can be created by specifying its type, format, dimensions, and usage. Here's an example of creating a 2D image object:

```cpp
VkImageCreateInfo imageCreateInfo = {};

imageCreateInfo.sType = VK_STRUCTURE_TYPE_IMAGE_CREATE_INFO;

imageCreateInfo.imageType = VK_IMAGE_TYPE_2D;

imageCreateInfo.format = VK_FORMAT_R8G8B8A8_UNORM;

imageCreateInfo.extent.width = width;

imageCreateInfo.extent.height = height;

imageCreateInfo.extent.depth = 1;

imageCreateInfo.mipLevels = 1;

imageCreateInfo.arrayLayers = 1;

imageCreateInfo.samples = VK_SAMPLE_COUNT_1_BIT;

imageCreateInfo.tiling = VK_IMAGE_TILING_OPTIMAL;

imageCreateInfo.usage = VK_IMAGE_USAGE_TRANSFER_DST_BIT | VK_IMAGE_USAGE_SAMPLED_BIT;
```

```
imageCreateInfo.sharingMode                                    =
VK_SHARING_MODE_EXCLUSIVE;

imageCreateInfo.initialLayout                                  =
VK_IMAGE_LAYOUT_UNDEFINED;

VkImage image;

vkCreateImage(device, &imageCreateInfo, nullptr, &image);
```

After creating an image object, memory must be allocated and bound to it. This involves querying the memory requirements and allocating the appropriate type of memory. Here's an example of memory allocation and binding:

```
VkMemoryRequirements memRequirements;

vkGetImageMemoryRequirements(device,                    image,
&memRequirements);

VkMemoryAllocateInfo allocInfo = {};

allocInfo.sType                                                =
VK_STRUCTURE_TYPE_MEMORY_ALLOCATE_INFO;

allocInfo.allocationSize = memRequirements.size;

allocInfo.memoryTypeIndex                                      =
findMemoryType(memRequirements.memoryTypeBits,
VK_MEMORY_PROPERTY_DEVICE_LOCAL_BIT);

VkDeviceMemory imageMemory;

vkAllocateMemory(device, &allocInfo, nullptr, &imageMemory);

vkBindImageMemory(device, image, imageMemory, 0);
```

Image views are created from image objects and describe how Vulkan should interpret the image data. Image views are essential for using images in shaders and for image layout transitions. Below is an example of creating an image view:

```
VkImageViewCreateInfo viewCreateInfo = {};

viewCreateInfo.sType                             = VK_STRUCTURE_TYPE_IMAGE_VIEW_CREATE_INFO;

viewCreateInfo.image = image;

viewCreateInfo.viewType = VK_IMAGE_VIEW_TYPE_2D;

viewCreateInfo.format = VK_FORMAT_R8G8B8A8_UNORM;

viewCreateInfo.subresourceRange.aspectMask       = VK_IMAGE_ASPECT_COLOR_BIT;

viewCreateInfo.subresourceRange.baseMipLevel = 0;

viewCreateInfo.subresourceRange.levelCount = 1;

viewCreateInfo.subresourceRange.baseArrayLayer = 0;

viewCreateInfo.subresourceRange.layerCount = 1;

VkImageView imageView;

vkCreateImageView(device, &viewCreateInfo, nullptr, &imageView);
```

Image layout transitions are necessary when an image's usage changes, such as from a transfer destination to a shader read. This can be done using a pipeline barrier. Here's an example of a layout transition:

```
VkCommandBuffer commandBuffer; // Assume command buffer is already created and started
```

```cpp
VkImageMemoryBarrier barrier = {};

barrier.sType                           =
VK_STRUCTURE_TYPE_IMAGE_MEMORY_BARRIER;

barrier.oldLayout = VK_IMAGE_LAYOUT_UNDEFINED;

barrier.newLayout                       =
VK_IMAGE_LAYOUT_TRANSFER_DST_OPTIMAL;

barrier.srcQueueFamilyIndex             =
VK_QUEUE_FAMILY_IGNORED;

barrier.dstQueueFamilyIndex             =
VK_QUEUE_FAMILY_IGNORED;

barrier.image = image;

barrier.subresourceRange.aspectMask     =
VK_IMAGE_ASPECT_COLOR_BIT;

barrier.subresourceRange.baseMipLevel = 0;

barrier.subresourceRange.levelCount = 1;

barrier.subresourceRange.baseArrayLayer = 0;

barrier.subresourceRange.layerCount = 1;

barrier.srcAccessMask = 0;

barrier.dstAccessMask = VK_ACCESS_TRANSFER_WRITE_BIT;

vkCmdPipelineBarrier(

commandBuffer,
```

```
VK_PIPELINE_STAGE_TOP_OF_PIPE_BIT,
VK_PIPELINE_STAGE_TRANSFER_BIT,

0,

0, nullptr,

0, nullptr,

1, &barrier
);

// Execute the command buffer to complete the transition

vkEndCommandBuffer(commandBuffer);

VkSubmitInfo submitInfo = {};

submitInfo.sType = VK_STRUCTURE_TYPE_SUBMIT_INFO;

submitInfo.commandBufferCount = 1;

submitInfo.pCommandBuffers = &commandBuffer;

vkQueueSubmit(queue, 1, &submitInfo, VK_NULL_HANDLE);

vkQueueWaitIdle(queue);
```

Using image objects and views efficiently is crucial for performance. It's important to manage image layout transitions and memory barriers properly to ensure synchronization and optimal usage of the GPU resources.

Samplers and Image Layouts

Samplers in Vulkan define how textures are sampled in shaders. They describe filtering, addressing modes, and other sampling parameters.

To create a sampler, you need to fill out a VkSamplerCreateInfo structure and call vkCreateSampler. Here's an example:

```
VkSamplerCreateInfo samplerInfo = {};

samplerInfo.sType = VK_STRUCTURE_TYPE_SAMPLER_CREATE_INFO;

samplerInfo.magFilter = VK_FILTER_LINEAR;

samplerInfo.minFilter = VK_FILTER_LINEAR;

samplerInfo.addressModeU = VK_SAMPLER_ADDRESS_MODE_REPEAT;

samplerInfo.addressModeV = VK_SAMPLER_ADDRESS_MODE_REPEAT;

samplerInfo.addressModeW = VK_SAMPLER_ADDRESS_MODE_REPEAT;

samplerInfo.anisotropyEnable = VK_TRUE;

samplerInfo.maxAnisotropy = 16;

samplerInfo.borderColor = VK_BORDER_COLOR_INT_OPAQUE_BLACK;

samplerInfo.unnormalizedCoordinates = VK_FALSE;

samplerInfo.compareEnable = VK_FALSE;

samplerInfo.compareOp = VK_COMPARE_OP_ALWAYS;

samplerInfo.mipmapMode = VK_SAMPLER_MIPMAP_MODE_LINEAR;

samplerInfo.mipLodBias = 0.0f;
```

samplerInfo.minLod = 0.0f;

samplerInfo.maxLod = static_cast<float>(mipLevels);

VkSampler textureSampler;

vkCreateSampler(device, &samplerInfo, nullptr, &textureSampler);

Image layouts are crucial in Vulkan, as they determine how the image data is organized in memory. When an image is created, it starts in an undefined layout, and it must be transitioned to the appropriate layout before it can be used. For instance, when you want to sample an image in a shader, you need to transition the image to VK_IMAGE_LAYOUT_SHADER_READ_ONLY_OPTIMAL.

Here's an example of transitioning an image layout for shader read:

VkCommandBuffer commandBuffer; // Assume command buffer is already created and started

VkImageMemoryBarrier barrier = {};

barrier.sType   = VK_STRUCTURE_TYPE_IMAGE_MEMORY_BARRIER;

barrier.oldLayout   = VK_IMAGE_LAYOUT_TRANSFER_DST_OPTIMAL;

barrier.newLayout   = VK_IMAGE_LAYOUT_SHADER_READ_ONLY_OPTIMAL;

barrier.srcQueueFamilyIndex   = VK_QUEUE_FAMILY_IGNORED;

barrier.dstQueueFamilyIndex   = VK_QUEUE_FAMILY_IGNORED;

```cpp
barrier.image = textureImage;

barrier.subresourceRange.aspectMask = VK_IMAGE_ASPECT_COLOR_BIT;

barrier.subresourceRange.baseMipLevel = 0;

barrier.subresourceRange.levelCount = mipLevels;

barrier.subresourceRange.baseArrayLayer = 0;

barrier.subresourceRange.layerCount = 1;

barrier.srcAccessMask = VK_ACCESS_TRANSFER_WRITE_BIT;

barrier.dstAccessMask = VK_ACCESS_SHADER_READ_BIT;

vkCmdPipelineBarrier(

commandBuffer,

VK_PIPELINE_STAGE_TRANSFER_BIT,
VK_PIPELINE_STAGE_FRAGMENT_SHADER_BIT,

0,

0, nullptr,

0, nullptr,

1, &barrier

);

// Execute the command buffer to complete the transition

vkEndCommandBuffer(commandBuffer);

VkSubmitInfo submitInfo = {};
```

```
submitInfo.sType = VK_STRUCTURE_TYPE_SUBMIT_INFO;

submitInfo.commandBufferCount = 1;

submitInfo.pCommandBuffers = &commandBuffer;

vkQueueSubmit(queue, 1, &submitInfo, VK_NULL_HANDLE);

vkQueueWaitIdle(queue);
```

Proper management of image layouts ensures that the GPU accesses the image data in the correct format, preventing undefined behavior and performance issues. It's also essential to synchronize access to image data to avoid race conditions.

In Vulkan, image samplers and image layouts work together to provide flexible and efficient texture sampling. Understanding these concepts is key to leveraging the full power of Vulkan for advanced rendering techniques.

Loading and Using Textures

Loading textures into a Vulkan application involves several steps, including reading the image file, creating Vulkan image objects, allocating memory, and transitioning image layouts. Here's a step-by-step guide to loading and using textures in Vulkan.

First, load the image file using an image loading library like stb_image.h:

```
int texWidth, texHeight, texChannels;

stbi_uc* pixels = stbi_load("texture.jpg", &texWidth, &texHeight, &texChannels, STBI_rgb_alpha);

VkDeviceSize imageSize = texWidth * texHeight * 4;
```

```cpp
if (!pixels) {

throw std::runtime_error("Failed to load texture image!");

}
```

Create a staging buffer to transfer the image data to the GPU:

```cpp
VkBuffer stagingBuffer;

VkDeviceMemory stagingBufferMemory;

createBuffer(imageSize,
VK_BUFFER_USAGE_TRANSFER_SRC_BIT,
VK_MEMORY_PROPERTY_HOST_VISIBLE_BIT                          |
VK_MEMORY_PROPERTY_HOST_COHERENT_BIT,
stagingBuffer, stagingBufferMemory);

void* data;

vkMapMemory(device, stagingBufferMemory, 0, imageSize, 0, &data);

memcpy(data, pixels, static_cast<size_t>(imageSize));

vkUnmapMemory(device, stagingBufferMemory);

stbi_image_free(pixels);
```

Create a Vulkan image object to store the texture:

```cpp
VkImage textureImage;

VkDeviceMemory textureImageMemory;

createImage(texWidth,                                    texHeight,
VK_FORMAT_R8G8B8A8_UNORM,
VK_IMAGE_TILING_OPTIMAL,
VK_IMAGE_USAGE_TRANSFER_DST_BIT                              |
```

```
VK_IMAGE_USAGE_SAMPLED_BIT,
VK_MEMORY_PROPERTY_DEVICE_LOCAL_BIT,
textureImage, textureImageMemory);
```

Transition the texture image to VK_IMAGE_LAYOUT_TRANSFER_DST_OPTIMAL and copy the staging buffer data to the image:

```
transitionImageLayout(textureImage,
VK_FORMAT_R8G8B8A8_UNORM,
VK_IMAGE_LAYOUT_UNDEFINED,
VK_IMAGE_LAYOUT_TRANSFER_DST_OPTIMAL);

copyBufferToImage(stagingBuffer,                    textureImage,
static_cast<uint32_t>(texWidth),
static_cast<uint32_t>(texHeight));

transitionImageLayout(textureImage,
VK_FORMAT_R8G8B8A8_UNORM,
VK_IMAGE_LAYOUT_TRANSFER_DST_OPTIMAL,
VK_IMAGE_LAYOUT_SHADER_READ_ONLY_OPTIMAL);
```

Create an image view and sampler for the texture:

```
VkImageView textureImageView = createImageView(textureImage,
VK_FORMAT_R8G8B8A8_UNORM);

VkSampler textureSampler = createTextureSampler();
```

Bind the texture image view and sampler to a descriptor set for use in shaders:

```
VkDescriptorImageInfo imageInfo = {};

imageInfo.imageLayout                                        =
VK_IMAGE_LAYOUT_SHADER_READ_ONLY_OPTIMAL;
```

```cpp
imageInfo.imageView = textureImageView;

imageInfo.sampler = textureSampler;

VkWriteDescriptorSet descriptorWrite = {};

descriptorWrite.sType = VK_STRUCTURE_TYPE_WRITE_DESCRIPTOR_SET;

descriptorWrite.dstSet = descriptorSet;

descriptorWrite.dstBinding = 1;

descriptorWrite.dstArrayElement = 0;

descriptorWrite.descriptorType = VK_DESCRIPTOR_TYPE_COMBINED_IMAGE_SAMPLER;

descriptorWrite.descriptorCount = 1;

descriptorWrite.pImageInfo = &imageInfo;

vkUpdateDescriptorSets(device, 1, &descriptorWrite, 0, nullptr);
```

In your fragment shader, sample the texture using the bound descriptor set:

```glsl
layout(binding = 1) uniform sampler2D textureSampler;

layout(location = 0) in vec2 fragTexCoord;

layout(location = 0) out vec4 outColor;

void main() {

outColor = texture(textureSampler, fragTexCoord);

}
```

Loading and using textures in Vulkan requires careful management of resources and synchronization. By following these steps, you can efficiently load and utilize textures in your Vulkan applications, enhancing the visual quality of your rendered scenes.

Chapter 8: Lighting and Shading

Basic Lighting Models

In computer graphics, lighting models are crucial for creating realistic images. They simulate how light interacts with surfaces. There are several basic lighting models commonly used in graphics:

1. **Ambient Lighting**: This is the simplest lighting model. It provides a constant illumination to all objects in the scene, simulating the effect of light scattered in the environment. Ambient light does not depend on the light's position or direction and is often used to ensure no part of the scene is completely dark.

2. **Diffuse Lighting**: Diffuse lighting simulates the scattering of light from a rough surface. It depends on the angle between the light source and the surface normal. The Lambertian reflection model is commonly used, where the intensity of the light is proportional to the cosine of the angle between the light direction and the normal.

```
float diffuseFactor = max(dot(normal, lightDir), 0.0);

vec3 diffuse = diffuseFactor * lightColor * objectColor;
```

1. **Specular Lighting**: Specular lighting models the reflection of light from a shiny surface. It creates highlights and depends on the viewer's position. The Phong reflection model is often used, where the intensity is proportional to the cosine of the angle between the reflection direction and the view direction, raised to a power (shininess factor).

```
vec3 reflectDir = reflect(-lightDir, normal);
```

```glsl
float spec = pow(max(dot(viewDir, reflectDir), 0.0), shininess);
```

```glsl
vec3 specular = lightColor * spec;
```

1. **Combined Lighting Model**: In practice, the ambient, diffuse, and specular components are combined to create realistic lighting. This combination is often represented in the Phong reflection model:

```glsl
vec3 phong = ambient + diffuse + specular;
```

1. **Directional Light**: This type of light simulates sunlight, where light rays are parallel and have a constant direction. Directional lights are often used for outdoor scenes.
2. **Point Light**: Point lights emit light in all directions from a single point, like a light bulb. The intensity of the light decreases with distance from the source.

```glsl
float distance = length(lightPos - fragPos);
```

```glsl
float attenuation = 1.0 / (constant + linear * distance + quadratic * (distance * distance));
```

```glsl
vec3 pointLight = (ambient + diffuse + specular) * attenuation;
```

1. **Spotlight**: Spotlights emit light in a specific direction and have a cone of influence. The light intensity decreases outside the cone.

```glsl
float theta = dot(lightDir, normalize(-spotDir));
```

```glsl
float epsilon = cutoff - outerCutoff;
```

```glsl
float intensity = clamp((theta - outerCutoff) / epsilon, 0.0, 1.0);
```

vec3 spotlight = (ambient + diffuse + specular) * intensity;

Understanding these basic lighting models is essential for creating realistic and visually appealing graphics. In the next sections, we'll delve into more advanced lighting techniques, including implementing the Phong shading model and shadow mapping techniques.

Implementing Phong Shading

Phong shading is a technique used in computer graphics to simulate the varying shades of color on a surface. It provides a more realistic rendering than flat or Gouraud shading by calculating the color at each pixel based on the surface's normal, light direction, and viewer direction. Phong shading involves three main components: ambient, diffuse, and specular lighting.

Phong Reflection Model

The Phong reflection model combines ambient, diffuse, and specular components:

1. **Ambient Component**: This provides a constant illumination to the surface, simulating indirect light.

vec3 ambient = light.ambient * material.ambient;

1. **Diffuse Component**: This simulates the light scattered in many directions when it hits a rough surface. It depends on the angle between the light direction and the surface normal.

vec3 norm = normalize(normal);

vec3 lightDir = normalize(light.position - fragPos);

float diff = max(dot(norm, lightDir), 0.0);

vec3 diffuse = light.diffuse * (diff * material.diffuse);

1. **Specular Component**: This simulates the reflection of light from a shiny surface. It depends on the angle between the reflection of the light direction and the view direction.

vec3 viewDir = normalize(viewPos - fragPos);

vec3 reflectDir = reflect(-lightDir, norm);

float spec = pow(max(dot(viewDir, reflectDir), 0.0), material.shininess);

vec3 specular = light.specular * (spec * material.specular);

Combining the Components

To achieve Phong shading, we combine the ambient, diffuse, and specular components:

vec3 result = ambient + diffuse + specular;

FragColor = vec4(result, 1.0);

Shader Implementation

Here is a basic implementation of Phong shading in GLSL:

#version 330 core

out vec4 FragColor;

in vec3 FragPos;

in vec3 Normal;

uniform vec3 lightPos;

```glsl
uniform vec3 viewPos;

uniform vec3 lightColor;

uniform vec3 objectColor;

void main()

{

// Ambient

float ambientStrength = 0.1;

vec3 ambient = ambientStrength * lightColor;

// Diffuse

vec3 norm = normalize(Normal);

vec3 lightDir = normalize(lightPos - FragPos);

float diff = max(dot(norm, lightDir), 0.0);

vec3 diffuse = diff * lightColor;

// Specular

float specularStrength = 0.5;

vec3 viewDir = normalize(viewPos - FragPos);

vec3 reflectDir = reflect(-lightDir, norm);

float spec = pow(max(dot(viewDir, reflectDir), 0.0), 32);

vec3 specular = specularStrength * spec * lightColor;

vec3 result = (ambient + diffuse + specular) * objectColor;
```

FragColor = vec4(result, 1.0);

}

Practical Tips

1. **Normal Vectors**: Ensure that the normal vectors are normalized before use, as their length affects the lighting calculations.
2. **Light and View Positions**: Update the positions of the light source and the camera/viewer in real-time to achieve dynamic lighting effects.
3. **Material Properties**: Adjust the ambient, diffuse, and specular properties of the material to achieve the desired appearance of the surface.

Phong shading is widely used in real-time rendering applications due to its balance between computational efficiency and visual realism. By understanding and implementing Phong shading, you can create more realistic lighting effects in your graphics applications.

Shadow Mapping Techniques

Shadow mapping is a technique used in computer graphics to add shadows to a 3D scene. It involves two main steps: rendering the scene from the light's perspective to create a depth map, and then using this depth map to determine whether a pixel is in shadow.

Step 1: Creating the Depth Map

First, we render the scene from the light's perspective and store the depth information in a texture. This texture is called the shadow map.

1. **Render Scene from Light's Perspective**: Set up a framebuffer

object (FBO) to render the scene from the light's point of view.

```
glGenFramebuffers(1, &depthMapFBO);

glGenTextures(1, &depthMap);

glBindTexture(GL_TEXTURE_2D, depthMap);

glTexImage2D(GL_TEXTURE_2D, 0,
GL_DEPTH_COMPONENT, SHADOW_WIDTH,
SHADOW_HEIGHT, 0, GL_DEPTH_COMPONENT,
GL_FLOAT, NULL);

glTexParameteri(GL_TEXTURE_2D,
GL_TEXTURE_MIN_FILTER, GL_NEAREST);

glTexParameteri(GL_TEXTURE_2D,
GL_TEXTURE_MAG_FILTER, GL_NEAREST);

glTexParameteri(GL_TEXTURE_2D, GL_TEXTURE_WRAP_S,
GL_CLAMP_TO_BORDER);

glTexParameteri(GL_TEXTURE_2D, GL_TEXTURE_WRAP_T,
GL_CLAMP_TO_BORDER);

float borderColor[] = { 1.0, 1.0, 1.0, 1.0 };

glTexParameterfv(GL_TEXTURE_2D,
GL_TEXTURE_BORDER_COLOR, borderColor);

glBindFramebuffer(GL_FRAMEBUFFER, depthMapFBO);

glFramebufferTexture2D(GL_FRAMEBUFFER,
GL_DEPTH_ATTACHMENT, GL_TEXTURE_2D, depthMap,
0);
```

glDrawBuffer(GL_NONE);

glReadBuffer(GL_NONE);

glBindFramebuffer(GL_FRAMEBUFFER, 0);

1. **Render Depth Information**: Render the scene, but only store the depth information.

glViewport(0, 0, SHADOW_WIDTH, SHADOW_HEIGHT);

glBindFramebuffer(GL_FRAMEBUFFER, depthMapFBO);

glClear(GL_DEPTH_BUFFER_BIT);

RenderSceneFromLightPerspective();

glBindFramebuffer(GL_FRAMEBUFFER, 0);

Step 2: Applying the Shadow Map

In the second step, we use the shadow map to determine whether each pixel in the scene is in shadow.

1. **Transform Coordinates**: Transform the coordinates of each pixel from the camera's view to the light's view and compare the depth values.

vec4 fragPosLightSpace = lightSpaceMatrix * vec4(fragPos, 1.0);

1. **Shadow Calculation**: Compare the depth of the current fragment with the depth stored in the shadow map.

float shadow = 0.0;

vec3 projCoords = fragPosLightSpace.xyz / fragPosLightSpace.w;

projCoords = projCoords * 0.5 + 0.5;

float closestDepth = texture(shadowMap, projCoords.xy).r;

float currentDepth = projCoords.z;

shadow = currentDepth > closestDepth ? 1.0 : 0.0;

1. **Combine with Lighting**: Combine the shadow factor with the lighting calculations to darken the areas in shadow.

vec3 lighting = (ambient + (1.0 - shadow) * (diffuse + specular)) * objectColor;

Example Shader Code

Here is a basic implementation of shadow mapping in GLSL:

#version 330 core

out vec4 FragColor;

in vec3 FragPos;

in vec3 Normal;

in vec4 FragPosLightSpace;

uniform sampler2D shadowMap;

uniform vec3 lightPos;

uniform vec3 viewPos;

uniform vec3 lightColor;

uniform vec3 objectColor;

```glsl
float ShadowCalculation(vec4 fragPosLightSpace)

{

vec3 projCoords = fragPosLightSpace.xyz / fragPosLightSpace.w;

projCoords = projCoords * 0.5 + 0.5;

float closestDepth = texture(shadowMap, projCoords.xy).r;

float currentDepth = projCoords.z;

float bias = 0.005;

float shadow = currentDepth - bias > closestDepth ? 1.0 : 0.0;

return shadow;

}

void main()

{

// Ambient

vec3 ambient = 0.1 * lightColor;

// Diffuse

vec3 norm = normalize(Normal);

vec3 lightDir = normalize(lightPos - FragPos);

float diff = max(dot(norm, lightDir), 0.0);

vec3 diffuse = diff * lightColor;

// Specular
```

vec3 viewDir = normalize(viewPos - FragPos);

vec3 reflectDir = reflect(-lightDir, norm);

float spec = pow(max(dot(viewDir, reflectDir), 0.0), 32.0);

vec3 specular = spec * lightColor;

// Shadow

float shadow = ShadowCalculation(FragPosLightSpace);

vec3 lighting = (ambient + (1.0 - shadow) * (diffuse + specular)) *
objectColor;

FragColor = vec4(lighting, 1.0);

}

Tips for Shadow Mapping

1. **Shadow Map Resolution**: Higher resolution shadow maps provide better quality shadows but at the cost of performance.
2. **Depth Bias**: Adjust the depth bias to avoid shadow acne and peter-panning artifacts.
3. **PCF (Percentage Closer Filtering)**: Use PCF to smooth the edges of the shadows.
4. **Cascaded Shadow Maps**: For large scenes, use cascaded shadow maps to improve shadow quality across different distances.

Shadow mapping is a powerful technique for adding realism to 3D scenes by accurately rendering shadows. By understanding and implementing shadow mapping, you can enhance the visual fidelity of your graphics applications.

Chapter 9: Performance Optimization

Profiling and Debugging Tools

Profiling and debugging tools are essential for optimizing Vulkan applications. These tools help developers identify performance bottlenecks and bugs, ensuring that applications run smoothly and efficiently.

One of the most widely used tools is **RenderDoc**, an open-source graphics debugger. RenderDoc captures single frames from Vulkan applications, allowing developers to inspect every aspect of the rendering pipeline. This includes shaders, draw calls, and resource bindings. By examining these details, developers can pinpoint inefficiencies and make informed decisions about optimization.

Another powerful tool is **NVIDIA Nsight**, which offers comprehensive profiling and debugging capabilities. Nsight provides detailed performance metrics, such as GPU utilization, memory bandwidth, and shader execution times. These metrics help developers understand where the application spends most of its time, enabling targeted optimizations.

AMD Radeon GPU Profiler is another valuable tool, especially for applications running on AMD hardware. It offers similar features to NVIDIA Nsight, including detailed performance metrics and shader analysis. By leveraging these tools, developers can optimize their applications for AMD GPUs.

To use these tools effectively, developers should integrate them into their development workflow. This typically involves running the application with the profiler attached, capturing performance data, and analyzing the results. It's important to profile the application under typical usage scenarios to obtain accurate data.

Here's an example of how to use RenderDoc with a Vulkan application:

```
// Initialize RenderDoc

RDCDriver driver = RDCDriver::Init();

driver.AttachToProcess(GetCurrentProcessId());

// Capture a frame

driver.StartFrameCapture();

RenderFrame(); // Your rendering code

driver.EndFrameCapture();
```

After capturing a frame, developers can open it in RenderDoc and inspect various stages of the rendering pipeline. This includes viewing draw call details, shader disassembly, and resource states.

In addition to these tools, Vulkan also provides built-in debugging features, such as validation layers. These layers can be enabled during development to catch common mistakes, such as invalid API usage or resource leaks. By addressing these issues early, developers can avoid performance pitfalls later.

Another useful feature is the **Vulkan Debug Utils Extension**, which allows developers to annotate their code with debug markers. These markers provide context in debugging tools, making it easier to correlate code with performance data.

Here's an example of using debug markers in Vulkan:

```
VkDebugUtilsLabelEXT label = {};
```

```
label.sType                                              =
VK_STRUCTURE_TYPE_DEBUG_UTILS_LABEL_EXT;

label.pLabelName = "My Debug Marker";

label.color[0] = 1.0f; // Red

label.color[1] = 0.0f; // Green

label.color[2] = 0.0f; // Blue

label.color[3] = 1.0f; // Alpha

vkCmdBeginDebugUtilsLabelEXT(commandBuffer, &label);

// Your rendering commands

vkCmdEndDebugUtilsLabelEXT(commandBuffer);
```

Using these tools and techniques, developers can systematically identify and resolve performance issues in their Vulkan applications. This leads to more efficient rendering and a smoother user experience.

Finally, it's important to stay updated with the latest versions of these tools, as they often include new features and improvements. Engaging with the community and sharing insights can also help developers learn new optimization strategies and best practices.

Pipeline Barriers and Memory Dependencies

Pipeline barriers and memory dependencies are crucial concepts in Vulkan for ensuring correct and efficient execution of rendering commands. They manage the synchronization of resource access, ensuring that operations occur in the correct order and that data is consistent across different stages of the pipeline.

A **pipeline barrier** is used to introduce a dependency between two sets of commands. This ensures that commands in the first set are completed before commands in the second set begin. Pipeline barriers can be used to manage various types of dependencies, including memory access, execution order, and resource transitions.

Here is an example of a simple pipeline barrier in Vulkan:

```
VkPipelineStageFlags                srcStageMask                =
VK_PIPELINE_STAGE_COLOR_ATTACHMENT_OUTPUT_BIT;

VkPipelineStageFlags                dstStageMask                =
VK_PIPELINE_STAGE_FRAGMENT_SHADER_BIT;

VkMemoryBarrier memoryBarrier = {};

memoryBarrier.sType                                             =
VK_STRUCTURE_TYPE_MEMORY_BARRIER;

memoryBarrier.srcAccessMask                                    =
VK_ACCESS_COLOR_ATTACHMENT_WRITE_BIT;

memoryBarrier.dstAccessMask                                    =
VK_ACCESS_SHADER_READ_BIT;

vkCmdPipelineBarrier(

commandBuffer,

srcStageMask,

dstStageMask,

0,

1,

&memoryBarrier,
```

```
0,

nullptr,

0,

nullptr
);
```

In this example, the pipeline barrier ensures that all color attachment writes are completed before any fragment shader reads occur. This is crucial for maintaining data consistency and avoiding race conditions.

Image layout transitions are another common use case for pipeline barriers. Images in Vulkan can have different layouts, and transitioning between these layouts requires careful synchronization. For example, an image might need to transition from a layout suitable for writing to one suitable for reading by a shader.

Here is an example of an image layout transition:

```
VkImageMemoryBarrier imageBarrier = {};

imageBarrier.sType                              = VK_STRUCTURE_TYPE_IMAGE_MEMORY_BARRIER;

imageBarrier.oldLayout = VK_IMAGE_LAYOUT_UNDEFINED;

imageBarrier.newLayout                          = VK_IMAGE_LAYOUT_TRANSFER_DST_OPTIMAL;

imageBarrier.srcQueueFamilyIndex                = VK_QUEUE_FAMILY_IGNORED;

imageBarrier.dstQueueFamilyIndex                = VK_QUEUE_FAMILY_IGNORED;
```

```cpp
imageBarrier.image = image;

imageBarrier.subresourceRange.aspectMask =
VK_IMAGE_ASPECT_COLOR_BIT;

imageBarrier.subresourceRange.baseMipLevel = 0;

imageBarrier.subresourceRange.levelCount = 1;

imageBarrier.subresourceRange.baseArrayLayer = 0;

imageBarrier.subresourceRange.layerCount = 1;

imageBarrier.srcAccessMask = 0;

imageBarrier.dstAccessMask =
VK_ACCESS_TRANSFER_WRITE_BIT;

vkCmdPipelineBarrier(

commandBuffer,

VK_PIPELINE_STAGE_TOP_OF_PIPE_BIT,

VK_PIPELINE_STAGE_TRANSFER_BIT,

0,

0,

nullptr,

0,

nullptr,

1,

&imageBarrier
```

```
);
```

In this example, the image transitions from an undefined layout to a layout suitable for transfer operations. The barrier ensures that any previous operations are completed before the transition.

Properly using pipeline barriers and managing memory dependencies can significantly impact the performance and correctness of a Vulkan application. It requires a thorough understanding of the rendering pipeline and careful planning of resource usage.

To avoid unnecessary synchronization overhead, developers should minimize the use of pipeline barriers and optimize the command submission order. Grouping commands with similar synchronization requirements and leveraging implicit synchronization points can help reduce the number of barriers needed.

In addition to pipeline barriers, Vulkan provides **events** and **semaphores** for more fine-grained synchronization. Events are lightweight synchronization primitives that can be set and waited upon by commands within the same command buffer. Semaphores, on the other hand, are used to synchronize command execution between different command buffers or queues.

Here's an example of using an event for synchronization:

```
VkEvent event;

VkEventCreateInfo eventCreateInfo = {};

eventCreateInfo.sType                                        =
VK_STRUCTURE_TYPE_EVENT_CREATE_INFO;

vkCreateEvent(device, &eventCreateInfo, nullptr, &event);

// Set the event
```

```
vkCmdSetEvent(commandBuffer,                              event,
VK_PIPELINE_STAGE_TRANSFER_BIT);

// Wait for the event

vkCmdWaitEvents(

commandBuffer,

1,

&event,

VK_PIPELINE_STAGE_TRANSFER_BIT,

VK_PIPELINE_STAGE_FRAGMENT_SHADER_BIT,

0,

nullptr,

0,

nullptr,

0,

nullptr

);
```

In this example, an event is set during a transfer operation and waited upon before executing fragment shader operations. This ensures that the transfer is complete before the shader reads the data.

By effectively managing pipeline barriers and memory dependencies, developers can optimize the performance and reliability of their

Vulkan applications, leading to smoother and more responsive graphics rendering.

Command Buffer Reuse and Optimization

Command buffer reuse and optimization are essential for achieving high performance in Vulkan applications. Command buffers encapsulate rendering commands and can be recorded once and executed multiple times, reducing CPU overhead and improving efficiency.

One of the key strategies for optimizing command buffers is **recording static commands** in advance. Static commands are those that do not change frequently, such as setting up pipeline states or binding resources. By recording these commands once and reusing the command buffer, developers can avoid the overhead of recording the same commands multiple times.

Here's an example of recording a static command buffer:

```
VkCommandBufferAllocateInfo allocInfo = {};

allocInfo.sType                                          = VK_STRUCTURE_TYPE_COMMAND_BUFFER_ALLOCATE_IN

allocInfo.commandPool = commandPool;

allocInfo.level = VK_COMMAND_BUFFER_LEVEL_PRIMARY;

allocInfo.commandBufferCount = 1;

VkCommandBuffer commandBuffer;

vkAllocateCommandBuffers(device, &allocInfo, &commandBuffer);

VkCommandBufferBeginInfo beginInfo = {};
```

```cpp
beginInfo.sType =
VK_STRUCTURE_TYPE_COMMAND_BUFFER_BEGIN_INFO;

beginInfo.flags =
VK_COMMAND_BUFFER_USAGE_SIMULTANEOUS_USE_BIT;

vkBeginCommandBuffer(commandBuffer, &beginInfo);

// Record static commands

vkCmdBindPipeline(commandBuffer,
VK_PIPELINE_BIND_POINT_GRAPHICS, graphicsPipeline);

vkCmdSetViewport(commandBuffer, 0, 1, &viewport);

vkCmdSetScissor(commandBuffer, 0, 1, &scissor);

vkEndCommandBuffer(commandBuffer);
```

In this example, the command buffer is recorded with static commands and can be reused multiple times during rendering.

Another important optimization technique is **secondary command buffers**. Secondary command buffers allow for more granular control and can be executed within primary command buffers. They are particularly useful for recording dynamic or frequently changing commands, as they can be re-recorded without affecting the primary command buffer.

Here's an example of using a secondary command buffer:

```cpp
VkCommandBufferAllocateInfo secondaryAllocInfo = {};

secondaryAllocInfo.sType =
VK_STRUCTURE_TYPE_COMMAND_BUFFER_ALLOCATE_INFO

secondaryAllocInfo.commandPool = commandPool;
```

```cpp
secondaryAllocInfo.level                            =
VK_COMMAND_BUFFER_LEVEL_SECONDARY;

secondaryAllocInfo.commandBufferCount = 1;

VkCommandBuffer secondaryCommandBuffer;

vkAllocateCommandBuffers(device,          &secondaryAllocInfo,
&secondaryCommandBuffer);

VkCommandBufferInheritanceInfo inheritanceInfo = {};

inheritanceInfo.sType                               =
VK_STRUCTURE_TYPE_COMMAND_BUFFER_INHERITANCE

inheritanceInfo.renderPass = renderPass;

inheritanceInfo.subpass = 0;

VkCommandBufferBeginInfo secondaryBeginInfo = {};

secondaryBeginInfo.sType                            =
VK_STRUCTURE_TYPE_COMMAND_BUFFER_BEGIN_INFO;

secondaryBeginInfo.flags                            =
VK_COMMAND_BUFFER_USAGE_RENDER_PASS_CONTINUE

secondaryBeginInfo.pInheritanceInfo = &inheritanceInfo;

vkBeginCommandBuffer(secondaryCommandBuffer,
&secondaryBeginInfo);

// Record dynamic commands

vkCmdBindDescriptorSets(secondaryCommandBuffer,
VK_PIPELINE_BIND_POINT_GRAPHICS, pipelineLayout, 0, 1,
&descriptorSet, 0, nullptr);
```

```
vkCmdDraw(secondaryCommandBuffer,                vertexCount,
instanceCount, firstVertex, firstInstance);
```

```
vkEndCommandBuffer(secondaryCommandBuffer);
```

```
// Execute secondary command buffer within a primary command
buffer
```

```
vkCmdExecuteCommands(primaryCommandBuffer,               1,
&secondaryCommandBuffer);
```

In this example, dynamic commands are recorded in a secondary command buffer and executed within a primary command buffer, providing flexibility and reducing re-recording overhead.

Command buffer recycling is another effective optimization technique. Instead of allocating and freeing command buffers frequently, developers can maintain a pool of pre-allocated command buffers and reset them for reuse. This approach minimizes memory allocation overhead and improves performance.

Here's an example of resetting and reusing command buffers:

```
vkResetCommandBuffer(commandBuffer, 0);
```

```
vkBeginCommandBuffer(commandBuffer, &beginInfo);
```

```
// Record commands
```

```
vkCmdBindPipeline(commandBuffer,
VK_PIPELINE_BIND_POINT_GRAPHICS, graphicsPipeline);
```

```
vkCmdDraw(commandBuffer,        vertexCount,        instanceCount,
firstVertex, firstInstance);
```

```
vkEndCommandBuffer(commandBuffer);
```

In this example, the command buffer is reset and reused for recording new commands.

By leveraging these techniques, developers can optimize command buffer usage in Vulkan applications, resulting in reduced CPU overhead, improved performance, and smoother rendering experiences.

Chapter 10: Advanced Vulkan Features

Geometry and Tessellation Shaders

Geometry and tessellation shaders are advanced stages of the Vulkan graphics pipeline that enable detailed and dynamic generation of graphics primitives. These shaders allow for the manipulation of vertices and geometry at a more granular level, providing opportunities for complex effects and optimizations.

Geometry shaders take primitives such as points, lines, or triangles as input and can produce new primitives as output. This stage is particularly useful for tasks like point sprite expansion, shadow volume extrusion, or geometry amplification.

To create a geometry shader in Vulkan, you need to follow these steps:

```glsl
#version 450

layout(triangles) in;

layout(triangle_strip, max_vertices = 3) out;

void main() {

for(int i = 0; i < 3; i++) {

gl_Position = gl_in[i].gl_Position;

EmitVertex();

}

EndPrimitive();

}
```

1.

```
glslangValidator -V geometry_shader.glsl -o geometry_shader.spv
```

1.

```cpp
VkShaderModuleCreateInfo createInfo = {};

createInfo.sType = VK_STRUCTURE_TYPE_SHADER_MODULE_CREATE_INFO;

createInfo.codeSize = sizeof(geometryShaderCode);

createInfo.pCode = (uint32_t*)geometryShaderCode;

VkShaderModule geometryShaderModule;

if (vkCreateShaderModule(device, &createInfo, nullptr, &geometryShaderModule) != VK_SUCCESS) {

throw std::runtime_error("failed to create geometry shader module!");

}
```

1.

```cpp
VkPipelineShaderStageCreateInfo geometryShaderStageInfo = {};

geometryShaderStageInfo.sType = VK_STRUCTURE_TYPE_PIPELINE_SHADER_STAGE_CREATE_

geometryShaderStageInfo.stage = VK_SHADER_STAGE_GEOMETRY_BIT;

geometryShaderStageInfo.module = geometryShaderModule;

geometryShaderStageInfo.pName = "main";

// Add geometryShaderStageInfo to the array of shader stages
```

1.

Tessellation shaders consist of two programmable stages: the tessellation control shader (TCS) and the tessellation evaluation shader (TES). These stages work together to subdivide patches into finer geometric details.

```glsl
#version 450

layout(vertices = 3) out;

void main() {

if (gl_InvocationID == 0) {

gl_TessLevelInner[0] = 3.0;

gl_TessLevelOuter[0] = 3.0;

gl_TessLevelOuter[1] = 3.0;

gl_TessLevelOuter[2] = 3.0;

}

gl_out[gl_InvocationID].gl_Position =
gl_in[gl_InvocationID].gl_Position;

}
```

    1.

```glsl
#version 450

layout(triangles, equal_spacing, cw) in;

void main() {

gl_Position = (gl_TessCoord.x * gl_in[0].gl_Position +

gl_TessCoord.y * gl_in[1].gl_Position +
```

```glsl
gl_TessCoord.z * gl_in[2].gl_Position);
}
    1.
```

```cpp
VkPipelineTessellationStateCreateInfo tessellationState = {};

tessellationState.sType                                        =
VK_STRUCTURE_TYPE_PIPELINE_TESSELLATION_STATE_CI

tessellationState.patchControlPoints = 3;
    1.
```

```cpp
VkPipelineShaderStageCreateInfo tessControlShaderStageInfo = {};

tessControlShaderStageInfo.sType                               =
VK_STRUCTURE_TYPE_PIPELINE_SHADER_STAGE_CREATE_

tessControlShaderStageInfo.stage                              =
VK_SHADER_STAGE_TESSELLATION_CONTROL_BIT;

tessControlShaderStageInfo.module = tessControlShaderModule;

tessControlShaderStageInfo.pName = "main";

VkPipelineShaderStageCreateInfo tessEvalShaderStageInfo = {};

tessEvalShaderStageInfo.sType                                  =
VK_STRUCTURE_TYPE_PIPELINE_SHADER_STAGE_CREATE_

tessEvalShaderStageInfo.stage                                 =
VK_SHADER_STAGE_TESSELLATION_EVALUATION_BIT;

tessEvalShaderStageInfo.module = tessEvalShaderModule;

tessEvalShaderStageInfo.pName = "main";
```

```
// Add tessControlShaderStageInfo and tessEvalShaderStageInfo to
the array of shader stages
    1.
```

Using geometry and tessellation shaders can significantly enhance the visual complexity and performance of your Vulkan applications. These shaders enable more detailed and dynamic graphics, allowing for advanced techniques like displacement mapping, adaptive tessellation, and procedural geometry generation.

Compute Shaders in Vulkan

Compute shaders in Vulkan provide a way to perform general-purpose computing on the GPU. Unlike traditional graphics shaders, compute shaders are not limited to the graphics pipeline and can be used for tasks such as image processing, physics simulations, and artificial intelligence.

```glsl
#version 450

layout(local_size_x = 256) in;

layout(binding = 0) buffer A {

float a[];

};

layout(binding = 1) buffer B {

float b[];

};

layout(binding = 2) buffer C {
```

```glsl
float c[];

};

void main() {

uint index = gl_GlobalInvocationID.x;

c[index] = a[index] + b[index];

}
```

1.

```
glslangValidator -V compute_shader.glsl -o compute_shader.spv
```

1.

```cpp
VkShaderModuleCreateInfo createInfo = {};

createInfo.sType                                    = VK_STRUCTURE_TYPE_SHADER_MODULE_CREATE_INFO;

createInfo.codeSize = sizeof(computeShaderCode);

createInfo.pCode = (uint32_t*)computeShaderCode;

VkShaderModule computeShaderModule;

if (vkCreateShaderModule(device, &createInfo, nullptr, &computeShaderModule) != VK_SUCCESS) {

throw std::runtime_error("failed to create compute shader module!");

}
```

1.

```cpp
VkPipelineShaderStageCreateInfo computeShaderStageInfo = {};
```

```cpp
computeShaderStageInfo.sType                                        =
VK_STRUCTURE_TYPE_PIPELINE_SHADER_STAGE_CREATE_IN

computeShaderStageInfo.stage                                        =
VK_SHADER_STAGE_COMPUTE_BIT;

computeShaderStageInfo.module = computeShaderModule;

computeShaderStageInfo.pName = "main";

VkComputePipelineCreateInfo pipelineCreateInfo = {};

pipelineCreateInfo.sType                                            =
VK_STRUCTURE_TYPE_COMPUTE_PIPELINE_CREATE_INFO;

pipelineCreateInfo.stage = computeShaderStageInfo;

pipelineCreateInfo.layout = pipelineLayout;

VkPipeline computePipeline;

if  (vkCreateComputePipelines(device,  VK_NULL_HANDLE,  1,
&pipelineCreateInfo,       nullptr,       &computePipeline)       !=
VK_SUCCESS) {

throw std::runtime_error("failed to create compute pipeline!");

}
```

1.

```cpp
vkCmdBindPipeline(commandBuffer,
VK_PIPELINE_BIND_POINT_COMPUTE, computePipeline);

vkCmdBindDescriptorSets(commandBuffer,
VK_PIPELINE_BIND_POINT_COMPUTE, pipelineLayout, 0, 1,
&descriptorSet, 0, nullptr);
```

```
vkCmdDispatch(commandBuffer,
(uint32_t)ceil(NUM_ELEMENTS / float(256)), 1, 1);
```

1.

Compute shaders are powerful tools for parallel computation on the GPU. They allow for efficient execution of data-parallel tasks and can be used to offload heavy computations from the CPU to the GPU, leading to significant performance improvements in various applications.

Ray Tracing with Vulkan

Ray tracing is a rendering technique that simulates the way light interacts with objects to produce highly realistic images. Vulkan provides support for ray tracing through extensions such as VK_KHR_ray_tracing_pipeline and VK_KHR_acceleration_structure.

```
// Ray Generation Shader

#version 460

#extension GL_EXT_ray_tracing : require

layout(set = 0, binding = 0) uniform accelerationStructureEXT topLevelAS;

layout(location = 0) rayPayloadEXT vec3 payload;

void main() {

vec3 origin = vec3(0.0, 0.0, 0.0);

vec3 direction = vec3(0.0, 0.0, -1.0);
```

```
traceRayEXT(topLevelAS, gl_RayFlagsOpaqueEXT, 0xFF, 0, 0, 0,
origin, 0.0, direction, 10000.0, 0);

}
```

1.

```
VkAccelerationStructureCreateInfoKHR accelInfo = {};

accelInfo.sType                                    =
VK_STRUCTURE_TYPE_ACCELERATION_STRUCTURE_CREATE

accelInfo.type                                     =
VK_ACCELERATION_STRUCTURE_TYPE_TOP_LEVEL_KHR;

accelInfo.flags                                    =
VK_BUILD_ACCELERATION_STRUCTURE_PREFER_FAST_TRAC

accelInfo.maxGeometryCount = 1;

accelInfo.pGeometries = &geometry;

VkAccelerationStructureKHR topLevelAS;

if (vkCreateAccelerationStructureKHR(device, &accelInfo, nullptr,
&topLevelAS) != VK_SUCCESS) {

throw std::runtime_error("failed to create acceleration structure!");

}
```

1.

```
// Closest-Hit Shader

#version 460

#extension GL_EXT_ray_tracing : require

layout(location = 0) rayPayloadInEXT vec3 payload;
```

```glsl
hitAttributeEXT vec3 attribs;

void main() {

payload = vec3(1.0, 0.0, 0.0); // Example: color the hit point red

}
```

1.

```cpp
VkStridedDeviceAddressRegionKHR raygenRegion = {};

raygenRegion.deviceAddress                                    =
getBufferDeviceAddress(raygenSBTBuffer);

raygenRegion.stride = shaderGroupHandleSize;

raygenRegion.size = shaderGroupHandleSize;

VkStridedDeviceAddressRegionKHR missRegion = {};

missRegion.deviceAddress                                      =
getBufferDeviceAddress(missSBTBuffer);

missRegion.stride = shaderGroupHandleSize;

missRegion.size = shaderGroupHandleSize;

VkStridedDeviceAddressRegionKHR hitRegion = {};

hitRegion.deviceAddress = getBufferDeviceAddress(hitSBTBuffer);

hitRegion.stride = shaderGroupHandleSize;

hitRegion.size = shaderGroupHandleSize;
```

1.

```
vkCmdBindPipeline(commandBuffer,
VK_PIPELINE_BIND_POINT_RAY_TRACING_KHR,
rayTracingPipeline);

vkCmdTraceRaysKHR(commandBuffer,           &raygenRegion,
&missRegion, &hitRegion, &callRegion, width, height, 1);
```

1.

Ray tracing in Vulkan enables the creation of photorealistic images by accurately simulating light interactions. This technique is essential for achieving high-quality visual effects in modern graphics applications, such as reflections, refractions, and global illumination. With the power of Vulkan's ray tracing extensions, developers can implement these advanced rendering techniques efficiently on supported hardware.

Chapter 11: Cross-Platform Considerations

Platform-Specific Extensions

When developing Vulkan applications, it's crucial to consider the platform-specific extensions that can optimize performance and enhance functionality. Vulkan, by design, is a cross-platform API, but each platform (Windows, Linux, macOS, Android, etc.) may offer unique extensions to leverage specific hardware or system capabilities.

Platform-specific extensions are additional functionalities provided by Vulkan implementations on certain platforms. These extensions enable developers to access features that are not part of the core Vulkan specification but are available on specific hardware or operating systems.

For example, on Windows, the VK_KHR_win32_surface extension allows Vulkan to interface directly with the Windows windowing system. This extension is essential for creating a Vulkan surface that can present images to a Windows window. Similarly, on Android, the VK_KHR_android_surface extension provides the necessary functions to present rendered images on an Android device.

```
// Example: Creating a Vulkan surface on Windows

VkWin32SurfaceCreateInfoKHR createInfo = {};

createInfo.sType                                    =
VK_STRUCTURE_TYPE_WIN32_SURFACE_CREATE_INFO_KH

createInfo.hwnd = hwnd; // Handle to the window

createInfo.hinstance = hInstance; // Handle to the instance
```

```cpp
VkSurfaceKHR surface;

if (vkCreateWin32SurfaceKHR(instance, &createInfo, nullptr, &surface) != VK_SUCCESS) {

throw std::runtime_error("Failed to create Vulkan surface on Windows");

}
```

Extensions can also be used to optimize performance on specific hardware. For instance, NVIDIA provides several extensions such as VK_NV_ray_tracing and VK_NV_mesh_shader that allow developers to utilize advanced features available on NVIDIA GPUs.

To use platform-specific extensions, you must first check for their availability. This can be done using the vkEnumerateInstanceExtensionProperties function, which lists all supported extensions. Once confirmed, these extensions can be enabled during instance or device creation.

```cpp
// Example: Checking for a platform-specific extension

uint32_t extensionCount = 0;

vkEnumerateInstanceExtensionProperties(nullptr, &extensionCount, nullptr);

std::vector<VkExtensionProperties> extensions(extensionCount);

vkEnumerateInstanceExtensionProperties(nullptr, &extensionCount, extensions.data());

bool extensionFound = false;

for (const auto& extension : extensions) {
```

```
if                          (strcmp(extension.extensionName,
VK_KHR_WIN32_SURFACE_EXTENSION_NAME) == 0) {

extensionFound = true;

break;

}

}

if (!extensionFound) {

throw            std::runtime_error("Required            extension
VK_KHR_win32_surface not found");

}
```

Understanding and utilizing platform-specific extensions can significantly enhance the performance and capabilities of your Vulkan applications. However, it's essential to handle these extensions with care, ensuring your application remains portable across different platforms.

When developing for multiple platforms, it's advisable to use preprocessor directives to include platform-specific code only when compiling for that platform. This practice ensures that your codebase remains clean and manageable.

```
// Example: Using preprocessor directives for platform-specific code

#ifdef _WIN32

// Windows-specific code

VkWin32SurfaceCreateInfoKHR createInfo = {};
```

```cpp
createInfo.sType                                    = VK_STRUCTURE_TYPE_WIN32_SURFACE_CREATE_INFO_KHR;

createInfo.hwnd = hwnd;

createInfo.hinstance = hInstance;

if (vkCreateWin32SurfaceKHR(instance, &createInfo, nullptr, &surface) != VK_SUCCESS) {

throw std::runtime_error("Failed to create Vulkan surface on Windows");

}

#elif defined(__ANDROID__)

// Android-specific code

VkAndroidSurfaceCreateInfoKHR createInfo = {};

createInfo.sType                                    = VK_STRUCTURE_TYPE_ANDROID_SURFACE_CREATE_INFO_KI

createInfo.window = androidWindow;

if (vkCreateAndroidSurfaceKHR(instance, &createInfo, nullptr, &surface) != VK_SUCCESS) {

throw std::runtime_error("Failed to create Vulkan surface on Android");

}

#endif
```

In conclusion, platform-specific extensions are powerful tools that allow Vulkan developers to optimize their applications for specific environments. By understanding and appropriately using these extensions, you can ensure that your Vulkan applications run efficiently across all target platforms.

Integrating Vulkan with Window Systems

Integrating Vulkan with various window systems is a critical aspect of cross-platform Vulkan development. Each operating system provides its own mechanisms and APIs for window management, and Vulkan must interface with these to present rendered images.

On Windows, the integration is achieved using the VK_KHR_win32_surface extension. This extension allows Vulkan to create a surface that can present images to a window created using the Win32 API. The process involves creating a VkSurfaceKHR object that acts as a bridge between Vulkan and the Win32 windowing system.

```cpp
// Example: Creating a Vulkan surface on Windows

VkWin32SurfaceCreateInfoKHR createInfo = {};

createInfo.sType = VK_STRUCTURE_TYPE_WIN32_SURFACE_CREATE_INFO_KHR;

createInfo.hwnd = hwnd; // Handle to the window

createInfo.hinstance = hInstance; // Handle to the instance

VkSurfaceKHR surface;

if (vkCreateWin32SurfaceKHR(instance, &createInfo, nullptr, &surface) != VK_SUCCESS) {

throw std::runtime_error("Failed to create Vulkan surface on Windows");
```

```
}
```

On Linux, Vulkan can interface with the X Window System using the VK_KHR_xlib_surface or VK_KHR_xcb_surface extensions. These extensions allow Vulkan to create surfaces that can present images to windows managed by the Xlib or XCB libraries, respectively.

```
// Example: Creating a Vulkan surface on Linux with Xlib

VkXlibSurfaceCreateInfoKHR createInfo = {};

createInfo.sType                                          =
VK_STRUCTURE_TYPE_XLIB_SURFACE_CREATE_INFO_KHR;

createInfo.dpy = xDisplay; // Pointer to the X display

createInfo.window = xWindow; // X window ID

VkSurfaceKHR surface;

if (vkCreateXlibSurfaceKHR(instance, &createInfo, nullptr,
&surface) != VK_SUCCESS) {

throw std::runtime_error("Failed to create Vulkan surface on Linux
with Xlib");

}
```

For macOS, the integration is achieved using the VK_EXT_metal_surface extension. This extension enables Vulkan to create surfaces that can present images to a window created using the Metal API.

```
// Example: Creating a Vulkan surface on macOS

VkMetalSurfaceCreateInfoEXT createInfo = {};
```

```
createInfo.sType                                              =
VK_STRUCTURE_TYPE_METAL_SURFACE_CREATE_INFO_EX

createInfo.pLayer = metalLayer; // Pointer to the Metal layer

VkSurfaceKHR surface;

if  (vkCreateMetalSurfaceEXT(instance,  &createInfo,  nullptr,
&surface) != VK_SUCCESS) {

throw std::runtime_error("Failed to create Vulkan surface on
macOS");

}
```

Android provides the VK_KHR_android_surface extension for integrating Vulkan with the Android windowing system. This extension allows Vulkan to create surfaces that can present images to Android's native window, typically associated with a SurfaceView or TextureView.

```
// Example: Creating a Vulkan surface on Android

VkAndroidSurfaceCreateInfoKHR createInfo = {};

createInfo.sType                                              =
VK_STRUCTURE_TYPE_ANDROID_SURFACE_CREATE_INFO_

createInfo.window = androidWindow; // Pointer to the native
window

VkSurfaceKHR surface;

if (vkCreateAndroidSurfaceKHR(instance,  &createInfo,  nullptr,
&surface) != VK_SUCCESS) {
```

throw std::runtime_error("Failed to create Vulkan surface on Android");

}

Integrating Vulkan with different window systems involves not only creating the surface but also handling various platform-specific events and synchronization mechanisms. For instance, on Windows, you need to handle window resize events to recreate the swap chain and associated resources.

// Example: Handling window resize event on Windows

void OnWindowResized(HWND hwnd, int newWidth, int newHeight) {

// Recreate the swap chain and associated resources

vkDeviceWaitIdle(device);

CleanupSwapChain();

CreateSwapChain(newWidth, newHeight);

CreateImageViews();

CreateFramebuffers();

}

Similarly, on Linux, handling window events involves integrating with the X Window System's event loop.

// Example: Handling window events on Linux with Xlib

void HandleXEvents(Display* display) {

XEvent event;

```
while (XPending(display)) {

XNextEvent(display, &event);

switch (event.type) {

case ConfigureNotify: // Window resize event

int newWidth = event.xconfigure.width;

int newHeight = event.xconfigure.height;

OnWindowResized(newWidth, newHeight);

break;

// Handle other events as needed

}

}

}
```

In conclusion, integrating Vulkan with various window systems is essential for creating cross-platform applications. Each platform provides specific extensions and mechanisms for this integration, and understanding these is key to ensuring that your Vulkan application can present rendered images correctly across all target environments.

Portability Tips and Best Practices

Ensuring portability in Vulkan applications is vital for reaching a broader audience across different platforms. While Vulkan is inherently designed to be cross-platform, there are several tips and best practices developers should follow to maximize portability and maintainability.

1. Use Platform-Agnostic Code

Whenever possible, write platform-agnostic code. Vulkan's core API is designed to be platform-independent, and by sticking to the core API, you can minimize platform-specific code.

```cpp
// Example: Platform-agnostic Vulkan instance creation

VkApplicationInfo appInfo = {};

appInfo.sType = VK_STRUCTURE_TYPE_APPLICATION_INFO;

appInfo.pApplicationName = "Vulkan App";

appInfo.applicationVersion = VK_MAKE_VERSION(1, 0, 0);

appInfo.pEngineName = "No Engine";

appInfo.engineVersion = VK_MAKE_VERSION(1, 0, 0);

appInfo.apiVersion = VK_API_VERSION_1_0;

VkInstanceCreateInfo createInfo = {};

createInfo.sType = VK_STRUCTURE_TYPE_INSTANCE_CREATE_INFO;

createInfo.pApplicationInfo = &appInfo;

VkInstance instance;

if (vkCreateInstance(&createInfo, nullptr, &instance) != VK_SUCCESS) {

throw std::runtime_error("Failed to create Vulkan instance");

}
```

2. Abstract Platform-Specific Code

When platform-specific code is necessary, encapsulate it within abstraction layers. This approach keeps your main codebase clean and makes it easier to manage platform-specific implementations.

```cpp
// Example: Abstracting platform-specific surface creation

class VulkanSurface {

public:

virtual VkSurfaceKHR CreateSurface(VkInstance instance) = 0;

};

#ifdef _WIN32

class Win32VulkanSurface : public VulkanSurface {

public:

VkSurfaceKHR CreateSurface(VkInstance instance) override {

VkWin32SurfaceCreateInfoKHR createInfo = {};

createInfo.sType                                    = VK_STRUCTURE_TYPE_WIN32_SURFACE_CREATE_INFO_KH

createInfo.hwnd = hwnd;

createInfo.hinstance = hInstance;

VkSurfaceKHR surface;

if (vkCreateWin32SurfaceKHR(instance, &createInfo, nullptr, &surface) != VK_SUCCESS) {
```

```cpp
    throw std::runtime_error("Failed to create Vulkan surface on
Windows");
    }

    return surface;
    }

};

#elif defined(__ANDROID__)

class AndroidVulkanSurface : public VulkanSurface {

public:

    VkSurfaceKHR CreateSurface(VkInstance instance) override {

    VkAndroidSurfaceCreateInfoKHR createInfo = {};

    createInfo.sType                                    =
VK_STRUCTURE_TYPE_ANDROID_SURFACE_CREATE_INFO_KI

    createInfo.window = androidWindow;

    VkSurfaceKHR surface;

    if (vkCreateAndroidSurfaceKHR(instance, &createInfo, nullptr,
&surface) != VK_SUCCESS) {

    throw std::runtime_error("Failed to create Vulkan surface on
Android");
    }

    return surface;
    }
```

```cpp
};
```

```cpp
#endif
```

3. Handle Window Events Appropriately

Window event handling varies across platforms, and it's essential to manage these events correctly to maintain a responsive application. For example, resizing a window typically requires recreating the swap chain and associated resources.

4. Use Feature Checks

Different hardware and drivers may support different Vulkan features and extensions. Always check for the availability of features and extensions before using them.

```cpp
// Example: Checking for extension support

uint32_t extensionCount;

vkEnumerateDeviceExtensionProperties(device, nullptr, &extensionCount, nullptr);

std::vector<VkExtensionProperties> extensions(extensionCount);

vkEnumerateDeviceExtensionProperties(device, nullptr, &extensionCount, extensions.data());

bool extensionSupported = false;

for (const auto& extension : extensions) {

if (strcmp(extension.extensionName, VK_KHR_SWAPCHAIN_EXTENSION_NAME) == 0) {

extensionSupported = true;
```

```
break;

}

}

if (!extensionSupported) {

throw std::runtime_error("Required extension VK_KHR_swapchain
not supported");

}
```

5. Test on Multiple Platforms

Regularly test your application on all target platforms. This practice helps identify platform-specific issues early and ensures that your application performs consistently across different environments.

6. Use Cross-Platform Tools and Libraries

Leverage cross-platform tools and libraries to simplify development. Libraries like GLFW, SDL, and others provide abstractions for window and input management, reducing the amount of platform-specific code you need to write.

```
// Example: Using GLFW for cross-platform window management

if (!glfwInit()) {

throw std::runtime_error("Failed to initialize GLFW");

}

glfwWindowHint(GLFW_CLIENT_API, GLFW_NO_API);

GLFWwindow* window = glfwCreateWindow(800, 600, "Vulkan
Window", nullptr, nullptr);
```

```
if (!window) {

throw std::runtime_error("Failed to create GLFW window");

}
```

7. Document Platform-Specific Code

Clearly document any platform-specific code and its purpose. Good documentation helps maintain the codebase and assists other developers in understanding the platform-specific implementations.

8. Use Continuous Integration

Set up continuous integration (CI) pipelines to automate building and testing your application on multiple platforms. CI tools can help catch platform-specific issues early and ensure code quality.

In conclusion, writing portable Vulkan applications requires careful consideration of platform-specific details and a structured approach to abstracting and managing these differences. By following these best practices, you can create robust and maintainable Vulkan applications that run smoothly across various platforms.

Chapter 12: Case Studies and Real-World Applications

Game Development with Vulkan

Game development with Vulkan involves leveraging the powerful capabilities of the Vulkan API to create high-performance, cross-platform games. Vulkan provides low-level access to the GPU, enabling developers to optimize rendering and achieve higher frame rates. Here's an overview of how Vulkan is used in game development.

Setting Up Vulkan for Game Development

Before you start using Vulkan for game development, ensure you have set up the Vulkan SDK and the necessary development environment. This includes installing the Vulkan SDK, setting up your IDE, and configuring the project to include Vulkan libraries and headers.

```cpp
#include <vulkan/vulkan.h>

int main() {

// Initialize Vulkan instance

VkInstance instance;

VkInstanceCreateInfo createInfo{};

createInfo.sType                                    = VK_STRUCTURE_TYPE_INSTANCE_CREATE_INFO;

if    (vkCreateInstance(&createInfo,    nullptr,    &instance)    != VK_SUCCESS) {

throw std::runtime_error("failed to create Vulkan instance");
```

```
}

// Your game loop and rendering code here

vkDestroyInstance(instance, nullptr);

return 0;
}
```

Rendering Pipeline in Games

The rendering pipeline is a crucial aspect of game development. Vulkan's pipeline architecture allows developers to configure various stages, such as vertex input, vertex shading, fragment shading, and output assembly. Each stage can be fine-tuned for optimal performance.

Managing Game Assets

Managing game assets like textures, models, and shaders is essential in game development. Vulkan provides efficient ways to load and manage these assets. Using descriptor sets and image samplers, you can handle multiple textures and other resources efficiently.

Implementing Game Physics

Game physics involves calculating movements, collisions, and interactions between objects in the game world. While Vulkan does not directly handle physics, it works seamlessly with physics engines like Bullet or PhysX. The results of physics calculations can be used to update the positions and states of game objects, which are then rendered using Vulkan.

Handling Input and User Interaction

Games rely heavily on user input, whether from keyboards, mice, game controllers, or touchscreens. Vulkan applications can use platform-specific libraries (like GLFW or SDL) to handle input and user interactions. These inputs are then processed to control game characters, navigate menus, or manipulate objects within the game.

Optimizing Performance

Performance optimization is critical in game development. Vulkan's explicit control over the GPU allows developers to implement various optimization techniques. For example, command buffer reuse and pipeline barriers can help in reducing CPU and GPU idle times, ensuring smoother gameplay.

Cross-Platform Development

One of Vulkan's strengths is its cross-platform capability. By adhering to Vulkan's standards and using platform-agnostic code, developers can create games that run on Windows, Linux, macOS, and even mobile platforms like Android.

Multiplayer and Networking

Implementing multiplayer functionality in games requires robust networking code. While Vulkan handles the rendering, networking is managed by separate libraries or custom networking code. Data received over the network, such as player positions and actions, needs to be integrated into the game's state and rendered using Vulkan.

Real-World Example: A Simple Vulkan Game

Let's look at a simple example of a Vulkan-based game. This game initializes a Vulkan instance, sets up a basic rendering pipeline, and draws a rotating triangle.

```cpp
#include <vulkan/vulkan.h>

#include <GLFW/glfw3.h>

// Initialization and setup code omitted for brevity

void drawFrame() {

// Acquire an image from the swap chain

vkAcquireNextImageKHR(device, swapChain, UINT64_MAX, imageAvailableSemaphore, VK_NULL_HANDLE, &imageIndex);

// Submit command buffer for drawing

VkSubmitInfo submitInfo{};

submitInfo.sType = VK_STRUCTURE_TYPE_SUBMIT_INFO;

submitInfo.commandBufferCount = 1;

submitInfo.pCommandBuffers = &commandBuffers[imageIndex];

vkQueueSubmit(graphicsQueue, 1, &submitInfo, VK_NULL_HANDLE);

// Present the rendered image to the screen

VkPresentInfoKHR presentInfo{};

presentInfo.sType = VK_STRUCTURE_TYPE_PRESENT_INFO_KHR;
```

```cpp
presentInfo.swapchainCount = 1;

presentInfo.pSwapchains = &swapChain;

presentInfo.pImageIndices = &imageIndex;

vkQueuePresentKHR(presentQueue, &presentInfo);

}

int main() {

// Initialization and setup code omitted for brevity

while (!glfwWindowShouldClose(window)) {

glfwPollEvents();

drawFrame();

}

vkDeviceWaitIdle(device);

// Cleanup code omitted for brevity

return 0;

}
```

Future Trends in Vulkan Game Development

As hardware evolves, Vulkan will continue to be a critical API for game development. Trends like ray tracing, virtual reality, and augmented reality will push Vulkan's capabilities further. Developers need to stay updated with the latest Vulkan extensions and best practices to leverage these advancements.

Scientific Visualization

Scientific visualization involves the graphical representation of scientific data to enable researchers to analyze and interpret complex datasets. Vulkan's high-performance rendering capabilities make it an excellent choice for creating detailed and interactive visualizations.

Setting Up the Visualization Environment

Before starting with scientific visualization using Vulkan, ensure you have set up the Vulkan SDK and the necessary development environment. This includes installing the Vulkan SDK, setting up your IDE, and configuring the project to include Vulkan libraries and headers.

```cpp
#include <vulkan/vulkan.h>

int main() {

// Initialize Vulkan instance

VkInstance instance;

VkInstanceCreateInfo createInfo{};

createInfo.sType                                    = VK_STRUCTURE_TYPE_INSTANCE_CREATE_INFO;

if (vkCreateInstance(&createInfo, nullptr, &instance) != VK_SUCCESS) {

throw std::runtime_error("failed to create Vulkan instance");

}

// Your visualization loop and rendering code here
```

```
vkDestroyInstance(instance, nullptr);

return 0;

}
```

Data Preparation and Management

In scientific visualization, the data to be visualized often comes from various sources such as simulations, experiments, or observational data. Preparing this data involves converting it into a format suitable for rendering, such as meshes or volume data. Vulkan provides efficient ways to handle large datasets, ensuring smooth visualization.

Implementing Visualization Techniques

There are several common techniques used in scientific visualization, including volume rendering, surface rendering, and particle rendering. Vulkan's flexibility allows developers to implement these techniques efficiently. For example, volume rendering can be achieved using 3D textures and custom shaders.

Interactive Visualization

Interactivity is a crucial aspect of scientific visualization. Users should be able to manipulate the view, zoom in and out, and interact with the data. Vulkan's efficient handling of input and real-time rendering capabilities make it possible to create highly interactive visualizations.

Rendering Large Datasets

Rendering large datasets is a common challenge in scientific visualization. Vulkan's explicit control over memory and resource management allows developers to optimize the rendering of large datasets. Techniques such as level-of-detail rendering and data streaming can be employed to handle large volumes of data efficiently.

Real-World Example: Visualizing Molecular Structures

Let's consider an example where we visualize molecular structures using Vulkan. The molecular data is loaded, processed, and rendered using Vulkan's rendering pipeline.

```cpp
#include <vulkan/vulkan.h>

#include <GLFW/glfw3.h>

// Initialization and setup code omitted for brevity

void drawMolecule() {

// Acquire an image from the swap chain

vkAcquireNextImageKHR(device, swapChain, UINT64_MAX, imageAvailableSemaphore, VK_NULL_HANDLE, &imageIndex);

// Submit command buffer for drawing

VkSubmitInfo submitInfo{};

submitInfo.sType = VK_STRUCTURE_TYPE_SUBMIT_INFO;

submitInfo.commandBufferCount = 1;

submitInfo.pCommandBuffers = &commandBuffers[imageIndex];

vkQueueSubmit(graphicsQueue, 1, &submitInfo, VK_NULL_HANDLE);

// Present the rendered image to the screen

VkPresentInfoKHR presentInfo{};
```

```cpp
presentInfo.sType = VK_STRUCTURE_TYPE_PRESENT_INFO_KHR;

presentInfo.swapchainCount = 1;

presentInfo.pSwapchains = &swapChain;

presentInfo.pImageIndices = &imageIndex;

vkQueuePresentKHR(presentQueue, &presentInfo);

}

int main() {

// Initialization and setup code omitted for brevity

while (!glfwWindowShouldClose(window)) {

glfwPollEvents();

drawMolecule();

}

vkDeviceWaitIdle(device);

// Cleanup code omitted for brevity

return 0;

}
```

Future Trends in Scientific Visualization

Scientific visualization will continue to evolve with advancements in hardware and software. Vulkan's support for ray tracing and compute shaders will enable more sophisticated visualization techniques.

Additionally, integrating virtual reality and augmented reality will provide new ways for researchers to interact with data.

Virtual Reality Applications

Virtual reality (VR) applications create immersive environments that allow users to interact with digital content in a three-dimensional space. Vulkan's high-performance rendering capabilities make it an ideal choice for developing VR applications, providing low latency and high frame rates essential for a smooth VR experience.

Setting Up Vulkan for VR Development

Before starting with VR development using Vulkan, ensure you have set up the Vulkan SDK and the necessary development environment. This includes installing the Vulkan SDK, setting up your IDE, and configuring the project to include Vulkan libraries and headers. Additionally, you will need VR-specific SDKs such as OpenXR or the SDK provided by the VR hardware manufacturer.

```cpp
#include <vulkan/vulkan.h>

#include <openxr/openxr.h>

#include <openxr/openxr_platform.h>

int main() {

// Initialize Vulkan instance

VkInstance instance;

VkInstanceCreateInfo createInfo{};

createInfo.sType                                              = VK_STRUCTURE_TYPE_INSTANCE_CREATE_INFO;
```

```cpp
if (vkCreateInstance(&createInfo, nullptr, &instance) != VK_SUCCESS) {

throw std::runtime_error("failed to create Vulkan instance");

}

// Initialize OpenXR instance

XrInstance xrInstance;

XrInstanceCreateInfo xrCreateInfo{};

xrCreateInfo.type = XR_TYPE_INSTANCE_CREATE_INFO;

if (xrCreateInstance(&xrCreateInfo, &xrInstance) != XR_SUCCESS) {

throw std::runtime_error("failed to create OpenXR instance");

}

// Your VR loop and rendering code here

vkDestroyInstance(instance, nullptr);

xrDestroyInstance(xrInstance);

return 0;

}
```

VR Rendering Pipeline

The VR rendering pipeline involves rendering scenes from two slightly different perspectives, corresponding to the left and right eyes, to create a stereoscopic 3D effect. Vulkan's flexibility allows developers to set up and manage the rendering pipeline efficiently for VR.

Handling VR Input

Handling input in VR involves tracking the position and orientation of the user's head and controllers. This data is used to update the virtual camera and interact with the virtual environment. Vulkan applications can integrate with VR SDKs to handle this input seamlessly.

Performance Optimization in VR

Performance optimization is critical in VR to ensure a smooth and immersive experience. Vulkan's explicit control over the GPU allows developers to implement various optimization techniques, such as reducing latency, optimizing frame rendering, and efficiently managing resources.

Real-World Example: A Simple VR Application

Let's consider a simple VR application using Vulkan and OpenXR. This application initializes Vulkan and OpenXR, sets up the VR rendering pipeline, and renders a basic scene.

```
#include <vulkan/vulkan.h>

#include <openxr/openxr.h>

#include <openxr/openxr_platform.h>

// Initialization and setup code omitted for brevity

void drawVRFrame() {

// Acquire an image from the swap chain

vkAcquireNextImageKHR(device, swapChain, UINT64_MAX, imageAvailableSemaphore, VK_NULL_HANDLE, &imageIndex);

// Submit command buffer for drawing
```

```cpp
VkSubmitInfo submitInfo{};

submitInfo.sType = VK_STRUCTURE_TYPE_SUBMIT_INFO;

submitInfo.commandBufferCount = 1;

submitInfo.pCommandBuffers = &commandBuffers[imageIndex];

vkQueueSubmit(graphicsQueue, 1, &submitInfo, VK_NULL_HANDLE);

// Present the rendered image to the VR headset

VkPresentInfoKHR presentInfo{};

presentInfo.sType = VK_STRUCTURE_TYPE_PRESENT_INFO_KHR;

presentInfo.swapchainCount = 1;

presentInfo.pSwapchains = &swapChain;

presentInfo.pImageIndices = &imageIndex;

vkQueuePresentKHR(presentQueue, &presentInfo);
}

int main() {

// Initialization and setup code omitted for brevity

while (true) {

// Poll VR events

// Your VR event handling code here

drawVRFrame();
```

```
}

vkDeviceWaitIdle(device);

// Cleanup code omitted for brevity

return 0;

}
```

Future Trends in VR Development

The future of VR development will be shaped by advancements in hardware and software. Vulkan's support for ray tracing, advanced shading techniques, and improved performance will enable more realistic and immersive VR experiences. Additionally, the integration of haptic feedback and improved tracking will enhance user interaction within virtual environments.